FROM BREAKDOWNS TO BREAKTHROUGHS

STORIES OF GREEN ZONE PSYCHOTHERAPY

DR. K. SOHAIL

BETTE DAVIS RN BN MN

Published in 2014 by Green Zone Publishing
A division of Dr. Sohail Medicine Professional Corporation
213 Byron Street South
Whitby, Ontario, Canada L1N4P7
T. 905-666-7253   F. 905-666-4397
Email: bettedavis@rogers.com
Website: www.greenzoneliving.ca

National Library of Canada Cataloguing in Publication

Sohail, K. (Khalid), 1952 -   Davis, B. (Bette), 1952 -
From Breakdowns to Breakthroughs/K. Sohail, B. Davis

ISBN – **978-1-927874-08-0**
    1.   Psychology, Psychotherapy
    2.   Interpersonal Relationships.   . I. Title.

Editing   Bette Davis
Textual Design   Deana Seymore
Cover Design: Shahid Shafiq

Printed and Bound in Canada

From Breakdowns to Breakthroughs

DEDICATED TO

Our patients who have trusted us

to walk with them through their journey.

You have always been our greatest teachers.

ACKNOWLEDGEMENT

We are so very grateful to Deana Seymore who blends caring for our patients and our office with the demands of so many creative projects.

Michael Thompson should win an award for his reliability and dedication in taking care of all of the details related to the printing process.

Over many years, we have had a special creative bond with Shahid Shafiq who not only designs the covers for our books but is a source of unwavering support for Green Zone and for us. He has always been one of our greatest cheerleaders.

Words of love and admiration are inadequate to express our appreciation for our family and friends, those we affectionately refer to as our family of the heart. The drive to make our relationships, and those of our clients, increasingly healthier is inspired by our family - Adriana, Angus, Wardah and Salman.

To our cherished friends, Sue and Ian, thank you for your endless support and for creating a light-hearted and joy-filled Green Zone Retreat for Bette each Friday night - we have truly won the friendship lottery!

CONTENTS

PREFACE

Dear Readers,

It is always a privilege to be a part of another project on mental health, particularly the Green Zone and especially with Sohail, my co-traveler on life's journeys.

Many who have read our books and attended our seminars, have asked about our creative relationship. We have known each other for 35 years having been introduced in 1978 at the Waterford Hospital in St. John's, Newfoundland. As young professionals, Sohail was a Resident in Psychiatry and I was a beginning Mental Health Nurse, we were both eager to be therapists and to be a part of a clinic, like Creative Psychotherapy Clinic. Since then, both of us have travelled different paths but came back together as colleagues, co-therapists, co-authors and life partners.

In our clinic, we not only teach the Green Zone concept to our clients but it is a core value and a central part of our clinic philosophy. We structure our therapies, meetings and schedule so that we and our staff are more likely to stay in the Green Zone. At home, Green Zone principles guide how we live, grow and resolve conflicts with our family.

Dr. K. Sohail/Bette Davis

People have also asked us how we work together as co-authors. Many co-authors have a rhythm that works for them. Ours is a rather unique collaboration that reflects our individual strengths and the strengths of our relationship. We usually begin with the goal of talking about and collaborating on the entire book, so that we each feel that we are a part of the whole book no matter who writes a particular chapter. If we feel it is not obvious who the speaker is in a particular chapter and it needs to be, we add the author's name under the title.

As always, it is our sincere wish that each book we write helps ever-increasing numbers of people to live their lives with purpose, joy and contentment.

Yours in the Green,

Bette

Part One

General Psychotherapy

Chapter One

Psychotherapy-The Art of Healing and Growth

Introduction

Psychotherapy has remained a mystery for professionals as well as lay people as it is subtle, experiential and very difficult to explain in a logical and rational way. It is as much of an art as a science. That is why I call Psychotherapy, the art of healing and growth. I am quite aware that healing and growth are abstract concepts and hard to explain in concrete terms.

In this book, we will reflect and share with you our experiences and observations as psychotherapists to give you a general idea of the whole process from the beginning to the end and the dilemmas patients and therapists face at different stages of therapy. Our hope is that after reading this book, you have some idea as to what to expect from the therapist and what the therapist might expect from you, so that you can enter therapy with an open mind and heart able to benefit from the therapeutic process.

It is the birthright of every human being to be happy and not suffer. There is no need to feel ashamed or embarrassed of seeking professional help to create a happy, healthy and peaceful lifestyle. The more you enjoy life, the more people around you will enjoy your company and the more you will have a happy family and exciting social life. Psychotherapy is an art that helps people to decrease their sufferings and promote their personal and social growth.

COMMON PRESENTING PROBLEMS

Over the decades I have met many patients who share in their first session, "Doctor, I am unhappy and I want to be happy. Since I do not know why I am unhappy, I do not know what to do to be happy. Can you help me?"

It is so sad that when I ask them, "For how long you have been unhappy?" many of them say, "All my life".

During my first session when I ask them about the emotional problems they have been struggling with, some of the more common answers I get are,

> "I feel anxious."
> "I have panic attacks."
> "I feel sad all the time.'
> "I have been depressed most of my life."
> "I feel very lonely."
> "I feel miserable at work."
> "I do not like myself."
> "I am unhappy in my marriage."
> "I hate my family."

Dr. K. Sohail/Bette Davis

"I wished I was never born."
"I do not want to die but I do not want to live either."
"Life is nothing more than suffering."

These are the patients who did not have any physical illnesses. Even after investigations by their family doctor, they were told their test results were with in the normal range. It was suggested that a Psychiatrist might have a better idea as to the problem. Many of them were told, "I do not know what is wrong with you and why you are unhappy. You need to see a psychiatrist. It might be all in your head."

Sometimes people who suffer from emotional problems feel ashamed as they feel they might be imagining things. I try to share with them that those emotional problems and mental illnesses are as real as physical illnesses, the difference is that they cannot be detected by blood, urine tests or x-rays. Many of the emotional problems are related to people's personalities and lifestyles and can be assessed more by personal interviews than by laboratory tests. It is as much related to the subjective meaning in life as to the objective conditions of life. In some mysterious way the physical and the mental, the subjective and the objective lives are all interconnected. In many cases, human beings who suffer emotionally do not know how to deal with their emotions. Many of them are very intelligent and find it hard to understand that their problems are emotional not intellectual and it is difficult for them to analyze them rationally and logically. Emotions have their own logic like the logic of dreams. The heart has a logic that the mind does not know. It is sometimes very frustrating for people with university degrees who can fix computer problems or can build bridges, to deal with their anxiety, depression and anger because to them these feelings are not logical and rational. The more they try to understand their feelings logically the more they feel frustrated and overwhelmed and rather than feeling better they feel worse. In many cases it gets so bad they have a breakdown and they are unable to work or socialize, or even get out of bed. In some cases, people are brought to see a doctor or a psychiatrist by their dear ones who see them suffering. Their sufferings have made them emotionally paralyzed. They feel desperate but do not know what to do about it. All the things they have tried have failed. They also realized that their emotional problems are affecting the whole family. The emotional problems of one person can easily affect others in the family, at work and in the community.

FIRST INTERVIEW

Having a first interview with a psychotherapist can be a stressful experience. To make it easier for our patients, Bette, my co-therapist, is in contact by phone with each person that is referred. She interviews them to ensure that psychotherapy will address their needs. She also provides information about the process of psychotherapy, refers them to our website or one of our books and answers their questions to reassure them. It is a significant advantage when someone comes into therapy having read about our approach and begun the process of healing.

The first interview at our Clinic usually lasts for an hour and is conducted by both us, which helps patients to make a smoother transition from the phone to a face to face interview.

In the initial session, the patient is encouraged to share his/her struggles while I make some notes for my assessment which is sent to the referring doctor. I share with the patient that Bette is my co-therapist and if the patient joined group therapy or we invited the spouse or other family members, Bette will join me in our group, marital or family therapy sessions.

During the first interview while we listen to their life story, we focus on making the patient feel respected and accepted. At the end, I ask the person to share their theory of why they are suffering. When they finish their story, I ask them if they want to ask us any questions. We want to create an atmosphere of a dialogue. Before the patient leaves, Bette and I offer our impressions of what they have shared, highlighting their strengths. We emphasize that we admire their courage to get therapy and take responsibility for their problems, in particular and life, in general.

During my assessment I keep seven factors in mind as they affect the process of therapy. These factors reflect the patient's capacity to change and grow in therapy.

1. AGE
It is my observation that young people do better in therapy as their personalities are still flexible. As people get older they have a tendency to become rigid. Some therapists do not accept patients for dynamic or intensive psychotherapy if they are in their late forties or older. In our practice we do not

place a restriction related to age if they are motivated to change.

2. INTELLIGENCE
For people to benefit from the psychotherapy experience they have to be of average intelligence so that they can understand the process and actively participate in it. In my opinion, people with low intelligence benefit more from behavior therapy than dynamic psychotherapy.

3. PSYCHOLOGICAL SOPHISTICATION
Psychotherapy is a psychologically sophisticated process and people who are psychologically sophisticated benefit from it more. These are the people who are curious about why they feel anxious, sad or angry and what they can do to change it. Those people who are intelligent but not psychologically sophisticated benefit less from psychotherapy.

4. EMOTIONAL FLEXIBILITY
Since therapy creates a change in people's personality and lifestyle, emotional flexibility is important. Some patients are more flexible than others. In my experience, people with obsessive compulsive, idealistic and perfectionist personalities have a tendency to be less flexible and have a harder time engaging and changing in therapy.

5. SIGNIFICANT RELATIONSHIPS IN THE PAST
Psychotherapy takes place in the context of a significant therapeutic relationship between the patient and the therapist. Those people who have experienced some type of healthy significant

relationship with either a parent, grandparent, teacher or friend in the past are more likely to connect with the therapist and engage in the process.

6. MOTIVATION

Motivation is one of the major factors that will dictate how much an individual will benefit from therapy. The more a person is motivated the more they change, learn and grow. Those who see a therapist because their spouse, relative or probation officer insisted on it usually do not benefit that much.

7. CONNECTION WITH THE THERAPIST

The final factor that I consider significant in my assessment is the connection with the therapist. The more the patient feels connected with us and the more we feel connected with the patient, the more is the likelihood for therapy to be successful. I find it amazing that in spite of many social, linguistic and cultural differences most patients feel connected and are inspired to work with us.

WORKING THROUGH THE PROBLEMS

Most patients we see do their major work in a year. They start to see me weekly for an hour for a few months and when they join the group psychotherapy sessions their individual sessions become less frequent. We tailor therapy according to the individual's needs. Many are involved in a combination of individual, marital or group therapy sessions. Some also may have family therapy sessions. It is our goal that our patients create and maintain healthy relationships.

SPOKEN AND WRITTEN WORDS

Psychotherapy is generally known as the *talking cure*. The psychotherapist and patient use words to share their thoughts and feelings, and such exchange has a therapeutic effect on the patient. Over a period of time, new and old emotional wounds heal and the patient grows as a person.

Being a poet and a writer I have also discovered the power of written words. That is why I encourage my patients to keep a diary or write letters highlighting their progress in therapy. I feel that therapy does not only happen during therapy sessions, it also happens during the time in between the sessions. Many times patients develop an insight or a realization that is significant in therapy and if they do not record it, they forget it. So I ask them to keep a regular diary and bring it with them when they come for their sessions. When they bring their diary and read parts of it in the sessions, they have an opportunity to discuss and explore some of their experiences and their reactions that took place in between the sessions.

As a therapist and a writer, I am fascinated with the healing power of words. Just in the last few months, two of my patients, who were in the early stages of therapy, developed the courage to verbalize their truth in a few powerful words. A fifty year old man, for the first time in his life, said in group therapy, "I am gay", while a fifty year old woman, also for the first time in her life, said in her individual session, "I was raped". Saying those three words was a turning point in their therapy. They felt comfortable enough in therapy to share their truth without worrying about being judged, humiliated or made fun of. In therapy when the therapist or other group members accept and respect them, that helps them in turn to accept and respect themselves.

As therapy progresses patients are able to share their deeper secrets and wounds that have been hurting them for years. They share their story of their sufferings and as they heal, they develop more self confidence and self worth and improve their self image. As their self esteem improves they are able to grow and explore their fullest potential.

One of the realities people discover in therapy is that the process of healing and growing is a complex process. The recovery is not linear. People take three steps forward and one step back. Sometimes when they take a step backwards they feel discouraged. That is the time I ask them to read their diary to see that even when they have taken a step backwards, they are still farther ahead of the beginning point from which they started their journey. I also share with them the analogy that when a car is stuck in the snow, sometimes we have to drive backwards and then forwards. Moving backwards and forwards helps to get unstuck.

Many people in therapy realize that they have learnt some unhealthy and self destructive patterns growing up in unhealthy families and communities. Group therapy provides them with an opportunity to become aware of such patterns and then break them so that they learn new and healthier patterns. In many cases such a process is slow and needs a lot of patience and endurance. Group therapy is effective in a way that the healing and growth of one person offers hope and inspiration to another person to keep on coming and working in therapy. Some people have to strike 99 times before the rock breaks at the 100th strike. When the rock breaks, the person realizes that the 99 previous strikes were not wasted.

In therapy people realize that their emotional crisis, while being painful, was also an opportunity to grow. Many told me that after therapy they reached a higher level of growth than they had before the crisis. So therapy did not just help them to heal, it also helped them to grow further towards their fullest potential. Many said, "I was living at 6 out of 10 before therapy. During the crisis I dropped to 3. And now after therapy, I am living at 8 out of 10."

When people heal and recover I ask them to decrease the frequency of appointments and move from active therapy to maintenance therapy. I reassure them that the door to our clinic is always open. I jokingly say that our clinic might have a long waiting list but it offers a life long membership. Some of our patients just come once or twice a year to share their progress and growth and their successes in life. Others come back to attend group therapy as guest patients and share their success story to inspire new members. Some of them write and volunteer their success stories and we add them to our website for others to read.

END OF THERAPY
There comes a time when a person is ready to say goodbye to us, to therapy and our clinic, as they feel healed and confident to deal with the dilemmas of life on their own. At that time, I sometimes share with them a letter I received from my therapist colleague who was in therapy herself and had written that letter for her therapist. I thought it was a wonderful gift for

a therapist as it reflects the mysterious but meaningful relationship between patient and the therapist. Let me end this chapter by sharing that letter with you.

LAST LETTER TO A THERAPIST

There was a small and old book. It was in a corner on a shelf in the library. Most of its pages were glued together, a few of them were torn. The cover was stained and one couldn't read the writer's name. No one knew its content. Sometimes people would glance at it but not bother to pick it up. Some would pick it up and promptly put it back in its place, while others would get curious about the writer's name but after useless efforts would give up.

One day you stepped into the library, you looked at the book, you turned it a few times trying to understand its origin, and to decipher the writer's name. You decided to discover its content. You took all the tools you had. You used all the tools you needed: water, a lot of water, pins, needles, threads, brushes. You related to every page like it was a masterpiece, you washed the glue, you let it dry, you added the missing words and only when the pages were complete did you put them in the original order, and you sewed one to the other. At the same time you were absorbed reading the story, paying attention to every simple word because every word was important to you. You were attracted by the big facts and by the small nuances as well. You learned the story and it had a big value for you. You understood its value. Now the book is complete, the story clear, with a beginning and an end. Now the book is ready to be read by the other people too.

Lois

Chapter Two

From Breakdowns to Breakthroughs

One day you wake up with a sense of unreality. Everything that looked real yesterday looks unreal today. Such a realization creates tension, distress and pain. But it is an emotional rather than physical pain as it is related to the emotional rather than the physical heart. It is a sign of heartache not heart attack, you might call it emotional angina.

In the beginning you try to ignore it and it goes away. But after a few days or weeks, it returns and you ignore it again. It goes away to come back again and again until you cannot ignore it any longer. Finally, one day you are forced to face it, deal with it and address it.

You gradually realize that your reality was actually an illusion and you experience the beginning of disillusionment. And right in front of your eyes your truth starts to slip away from your fingers, from your heart and from your mind. You start to see cracks in the ceiling, in the walls and in the floor of your ideals, your passions, and your dreams. You realize that your truth was just *a* truth and not *the* truth.

And it can happen in any aspect of your life: physical, emotional, social, romantic, professional, ideological or existential. Gradually, the cracks become bigger and bigger and finally the tall stable building of your health or happiness, success or love, peace or faith starts to crumble and you experience a crisis. Finally, you have a broken heart and you experience a breakdown.

Some people who experience a breakdown feel so pessimistic that they commit suicide. Some suffer all their lives and never recover, while others, who reflect and introspect, develop insights and foresights, get support from their friends and guidance from their therapists, in time transform their breakdowns into breakthroughs. How fortunate are those people!

Chapter Three

To Die or Not to Die?

Part One — The Last Letter

Hazel's letter was the first suicide letter I had ever received from a patient. It was Hazel's last, written as she contemplated cutting her throat with a sharp knife. It read:

> *Dear Dr. Sohail*
> *Couldn't leave without saying goodbye and thanking you for all you have tried to do for me.*
> *I was never meant to be. My story was never meant to be told.*
> *Sitting at this dirty beach but there are loons, ducks, gulls and other assorted birds. They are making the best of a bad situation but I cannot.*
> *My van battery is dead now because I left my lights on. This too was meant to be.*
> *Please do not think I took the easy way out. This is my bravest act yet and something I must do.*

I can't bear to be here anymore.
No angels for me. Not this time.
Thank- you for all you do
My best always
Hazel

PART TWO — A CONCERNED PHONE CALL

It was 5:30 p.m. and I was about to leave the clinic when my secretary, Deana told me that there was a distressed young woman on the phone who desperately wanted to talk to me. I picked up the phone and said,

"I am Dr Sohail. How can I help you?"
"My name's Amy" she said, "And I am Brian's girlfriend, who is your patient Hazel's son." Then there was a long pause. It sounded as if she was choking with emotion. I wondered why she had called me.

"Go ahead, tell me what's happening."
"Today is Hazel's birthday." She continued. "We came with a gift to give her a surprise but we got a surprise instead."

"What kind of surprise?"
"She is missing and she left a suicide note."

"Who is it addressed to?"
"It is addressed to her husband, Mark. What do you suggest we do now?"

"It's a sad situation. I would suggest that you call the police so that they can find her and take her to

the emergency department for a psychiatric assessment."

"Brian and I are worried she would get mad at us for calling the police."
"Don't worry. You can tell her that I had suggested it. She will forgive me as she has a good relationship with me. We are doing this out of concern for her."

"Thank you, Dr. Sohail. I really appreciate your support."
"I hope the police can find her before she hurts herself. One more thing before I go, can you fax me that suicide note?"
"Sure."

Hazel was one of the gentlest and kindest women I had known. She was a Native Indian and was very generous. She had recently returned from the USA after breaking up with her husband and she was broken hearted. Her dream of a loving future with her husband had turned into a nightmare.

The next morning when I woke up I had no idea whether I would ever see Hazel again. I went to the clinic with a heavy heart. I found a fax from Amy. It was Hazel's letter to Mark. It said,

> *"Dear Mark, It is April 7th, my birthday and it seems like a good day to finalize this letter to you. I wrote it some time ago...shortly after I received the Divorce Petition from you. Since that time I wrestled with living or dying and*

now, on this day, I know that I have no other choice.

Congratulations! You have managed to beat me down...I can't handle feeling so rejected, nor go through any more struggles or abandonment...from you or anyone else...I just can't do it any longer.

I can't and won't fight you in court. I begged for some more time to get myself together and you will not abide it. You want your pound of flesh. You now have it. All of it. There is nothing left of me but heartache and pain...rejection and abandonment.

I don't care to live any more.

The letter ended with the following paragraph.

I hope that this is not too "drawn out" for you...these are my final words to you ever...I truly believed that we could be Mr. and Mrs. Twoclouds for evermore and I wish that these were words of undying love instead of just "dying"...

I am done.

Mrs. Twoclouds

Reading that letter, I remembered a case that Sigmund Freud had discussed with his colleagues. A woman who was abandoned by her husband had killed herself. Others said she had committed suicide but Freud insisted that she had committed homicide as she hated her husband and wanted to kill him; but she had emotionally internalized him so much that the only way to kill him was to kill herself. I wondered whether Hazel had contemplated suicide or homicide.

In the afternoon I was relieved to learn that Hazel had returned home at 2 a.m. and had been taken to the hospital by her family and police and had been kept there for a few hours. She was seen by a psychiatrist who knew me, and discharged her back into my care.

The next day when I saw her she brought three letters that she had written while she was contemplating suicide. I was quite touched by the letter she had written to her sister, Laura. It stated,

> *Dear Laura,*
> *I can't thank you enough for being there for me in every way. You have been my staunchest supporter and I love you so much.*
> *I wish I could be stronger but I am not.*
> *Too many obstacles. Too much rejection.*
> *My kids hurt so badly and can't deal with me. Neither can the rest of the family. I hurt for them all.*
> *I can't hang on.*
> *I left the last of my American money for you. I hope it helps a little.*
> *Left Rose her $300 loan repayment, too. Please make sure she receives it and thank her for her support.*
> *I am so grateful to you.*
> *Sorry that I could not hang on but I just can't.*
> *Thank you for all of your love, my sister.*
> *I love you*
> *Hazel*

I offered her support and suggested that I meet with her family to process this whole episode. She agreed.

A few days later I met with her three sisters, one brother, two sons, the son's girlfriend who had called me and her daughter. They shared their thoughts and feelings. I was impressed by their caring and compassion. It was obvious that Hazel was connected with some family members more than others. Her suicide attempt was a wake-up call and they were open to learning how they could offer more support. They did not realize how hurt she had felt by her marital break-up. They always saw her as a strong person who provided support to others. Now that she was weak, the one who was fragile and vulnerable she did not know how to ask for help and they did not know how to offer it. That meeting was very productive as it helped them share their feelings and start a new chapter of their family life. In the end Hazel thanked them for becoming part of her healing and recovery.

PART THREE – INTERVIEW WITH HAZEL
When Hazel had reasonably recovered, I asked if I could tape an interview about her crisis. She readily agreed.

Sohail: *Thank you for agreeing to be interviewed. Can you recollect what was happening in your life when you felt at your lowest on your return from the USA?*
Hazel: When I first got back to Canada I was in shock, I was in survival mode. I needed a lot of support but it wasn't there at all. There were a number of factors that were very stressful for me.

The first one was my mother, who lives downstairs in the basement. She is an extremely negative person. It is not only that she is not supportive, she also damages others with her criticisms. She ridicules and finds faults not just in me but in everyone. I found it very, very, very depressing.

The second one was my divorce. When Mark served me with divorce papers, I was in no position to financially afford a Missouri lawyer or fly to Missouri to defend myself. So a paralegal friend of my sister's volunteered to help me. She promised to build a strong case but I could not find her. It was rather frustrating as she did not return my calls or respond to my emails. Then she started treating me as if I was a mental case. She was condescending in her approach. She wanted me to go on welfare.

One day a friend of mine volunteered to take me to the welfare department. I even confirmed it the day before. But when I called her she was gone. I felt vulnerable and nervous. When I went to see that welfare worker for my interview on my own, she was extremely judgmental, criticizing my life. She told me I should have never married somebody from the States as I didn't know that person well. She was very judgmental. I felt like saying, 'It's none of your business," but I kept quiet. She said I did not qualify because I had Mark's van. It was the last straw.

I suddenly realized that my friend let me down, my kids were not there to help me, my mother was emotionally abusive and finally the welfare woman insulted me and I felt like an idiot. I felt like an emotional boil that was ready to burst.

Sohail: *What motivated you to write the letters?*
Hazel: I wanted to leave instructions for the police and I wanted to return $300 to an elderly lady who had lent me the money when I needed it. I also wanted to write a letter to my sister and my children and also to you before I killed myself.

Sohail: *What time did you leave home?*
Hazel: I think it was 9 or 9:30 a.m. on my birthday.

Sohail: *Why was it important for you to do it on your birthday?*
Hazel: I wasn't sure whether anybody would acknowledge it or not. If they didn't, I didn't want to know and there just didn't seem any point to life.

Sohail: *You had also mentioned that you took a knife.*
Hazel: Yes.

Sohail: *From the kitchen or somewhere else?*
Hazel: It was from a toolbox. It was a very wide, big utility knife. I thought it was so sharp that it would be the best.

Sohail: *How you were going to use that knife?*
Hazel: I was going to slit my throat. I've been feeling my neck for days to feel where the arteries were so I could make sure I didn't just slice the skin and bleed. I wanted to find at least one of those major arteries so that I could slice my throat and bleed in a minute or two. I didn't want to do it at my home and leave that mess. I did not want it to be a reminder for others.

Sohail: *Where did you want to go?*

Hazel: I just wanted to go somewhere where I wouldn't be noticed. I did not want to be found out before I died.

Sohail: *So when you left home, where did you go first?*
Hazel: I went to the lake in Courtice, down to this side road with this dirty little beach and it was raining. There were big potholes full of water. I was trying to find the Courtice Conservation Area. It had been many, many years since I had been there. So I could not remember and kept on going and I came up to this dirty little beach that had a little strip of parking in the area. So I just sat for a while and I was thinking about my children and other people I cared for. I thought I also needed to leave these instructions because if the police found my body they would not know where to take it as my van had a Missouri plate.

Sohail: *So you wrote the letters at the beach?*
Hazel: I wrote the first one for the instructions and then I thought I should write to my children and then I needed to write to you. At first I was very, very calm. I wasn't crying or distressed. I was very, very calm. The problem was people kept coming there and parking. I didn't want to be seen or caught so I was buying time waiting to be alone. It was a rainy miserable day but still people kept on coming, mostly men of different ages.

Then I had another problem. I had left my lights on without realizing it and I started to get cold. So when I wanted to turn on the motor so that I could get some heat, I discovered that the battery was dead. That confirmed to me that this was meant to be and I was supposed to stay there and I was supposed to do this because I had no way to leave now.

But then people just kept on coming and coming and coming and it ended up not to be a very private place. It really mattered to me that nobody found me. I did not want to survive. Then a young couple came and parked beside me and they went for a little walk and when they came back I asked them if they had booster cables, if they could boost my van because I wanted to go somewhere else and I had to pee and I wanted to get warm. She said she did not have any but she would go home and get cables and bring them back to give me a boost. I asked her if she was sure and she said, "Yes". I did not believe her but she came back in 20 minutes. Then they could not open the hood of their car and another man helped them. They undid the hood and then boosted my battery. I kept thanking them and she said "No problem, if it happened to me I would want someone helping me." Then she said "But before I go could I give you a hug because you sure look like you need one."

So I couldn't shut the vehicle off because I needed it to charge so I got on the 401 and I drove to the service station at Port Hope. That's a very busy one because there is a Swiss Chalet and other stores and people keep on coming and going in that plaza. I thought I might do it there and nobody would see me but I could not get the courage to do it. All day long I just kept on trying to work up the courage to do it but could not. I needed to evoke violence because I was trying but it was not cutting me. It was scratching but it was not slicing my neck. I knew I had to plunge it in and really I wasn't in that frame of mind. I couldn't conjure up violence and then I thought it was so stinky there from the fumes from the trucks and the buses' diesel fuel and it was sickening and I thought I don't want to die in a stinky place like this.

I was driving around up these side roads, there was a driving spot end near there that I used to take my children when they were young and it was closed. I went there and I tried it again and I just couldn't get it to cut me and then I went up just another road that ended at a person's driveway so I couldn't be there. I just kept on trying to find the right place and then trying to conjure up the courage. I needed to be violent. Then I went to a little parkette in Port Hope but there was a couple in the car. My fear was that somebody would find me before I was dead. I needed to know that I was going to cut that main artery and I needed a few minutes to bleed out, so I smoked cigarettes waiting for them to go and then it got dark and I heard somebody come and get into a car. I struggled with getting caught. I didn't want to get caught before I was dead. I kept saying, "Just do it, if you did it when you got here it would be over, you would be dead." I kept saying, "Just do it, if you had done it, it would be over," but I just couldn't and yet as the day wore on and I was so determined, I just couldn't do it. And then I went to a different service station on the way back to Oshawa in the pouring rain and it was getting dark. It said it was a 20 minute parking limit and I thought I would have to do it right away because they do watch the parking lot. I tried on my throat and I couldn't do it and then I tried to slit my wrist. I thought it would take longer but if I slit both of the wrists and keep my arms down they will bleed. But there were two bones on each side and it wouldn't go and again I guess I would have to plunge it in between the bones. I couldn't do that to a turtle or a bug so I guess I couldn't conjure up enough violence. It wasn't a matter of not wanting to die or not being determined. I just could not be so violent to stab my neck with a sharp knife.

Sohail: *So when did you finally decide that you needed to go home?*
Hazel: When I sliced my wrist and it didn't bleed and it was very, very late, it was about one or two in the morning or whatever. I went home and I thought there would probably be nobody there. Brian might be there and if he was, I was going to show him the knife and tell him what I have done, but I just needed to go home and go to bed and rest. I needed to take a sleeping pill and sleep. I didn't want to take an overdose. I just needed to go to sleep. I wanted to go to bed and go to sleep hoping tomorrow will be different. When I got home everybody was there and they had called the police and I just kept telling them what I had done. My sister, Sarah came out of the house and put her arms around me and said, "Thank God, thank God, I've been praying". She reassured me by saying, "It's ok and we are all here and we are all going to help you. We are all going to help you, its ok." My other two sisters came out and they didn't say anything. The younger sister patted me on the back and said, "It's going to get better." Then I went inside and the police came and told me that we had to go to the hospital. I felt so bad that I had put all these people out and the police were looking all day. I kept on saying I was sorry.

Sohail: *How long were you in the hospital?*
Hazel: Just till the morning.

Sohail: *What did the doctor do?*
Hazel: The nurses put me in a little room and we talked and it was an hour or two before the doctor came. He had a clipboard. He was asking quick questions and I found it really annoying and I didn't want to be there because I know hospitals don't like people who want to commit suicide. They avoid you as it pisses them off. He just asked horrible questions.

Sohail: *He wasn't very sensitive.*
Hazel: No, not at all. I really resented the questions and I resented answering because I thought it was just a formality. He was asking things off the clip board, he did not give a shit. I thought "Hurry up and do it and say good bye." They took me into this room that looked like a prison cell and said I had to stay the night and there was a female guard there. My son and his girlfriend and my sister stayed until probably about 7 a.m. and then they went home for a few hours to sleep. In the morning a lady from the Distress Centre came in and asked me a lot of personal questions about my life and my emotional pain but she was compassionate and she used the answers to create a dialogue, rather than clip board questions. Then she said that she would go to the psychiatrist and relay the circumstances of my story to him. She said, "It's obvious that you're not insane, you are not schizophrenic and your crisis is circumstantial." Eventually the psychiatrist came and asked me if I was on anti-depressants. He knew you and asked me to make another appointment with you for follow up.

Sohail: *He let you go home?*
Hazel: Yes. They let me go home but they said I have to be supervised. My sister agreed to stay in my house with me for two weeks.

Sohail: *You seem to be improving now.*
Hazel: I am feeling better. My sister and my children are supporting me.

Sohail: *Did something good come out of it?*
Hazel: Yes, I know how much my family cares for me. And I have decided to simplify my life. I no longer want to be part of a rat race.

Sohail: *How do you see your emotional breakdown now?*
Hazel: Tension kept on building up. There was no release or relief. There was an emotional boil that finally burst.

PART FOUR — REFLECTIONS
When I reflect on Hazel's interview and story, the following significant aspects come to my mind:

1.   MOTHER WITH NO EMOTIONAL ARMS
When Hazel came back from the USA she was broken-hearted and needed some tender loving care to heal and recover. She was hoping to get some support from her mother but unfortunately her mother was so involved in her own pains and miseries that she could not offer any support to her daughter. Hazel's story reminded me of the writer Virginia Woolf, who killed herself at the age of 59 by filling her coat pockets with rocks and walking into the river near her home. Woolf had had a number of

depressive episodes in her life. The first was at age 13 after the death of her mother. Woolf wrote in her diary later on that her mother could not hug her because she had no emotional arms. Hazel had the same dilemma. Her mother had no emotional arms either. She was neither motherly, nor nurturing and could not help her daughter when she was in an emotional crisis and needed her the most.

2. LEGAL BATTLE

While Hazel was recovering from the rejection and abandonment by her husband, he sent her divorce papers. It was like rubbing salt in her wounds. Her feelings were still raw and she could not handle that. She wanted some time to heal from the emotional wounds before she dealt with the legal situation but her husband insisted. A paralegal friend of her sister promised to help but did not fulfill her promise. Hazel was worried that if she did not comply with the legal requirements, she would not receive any financial support from her husband. Her financial worries added to her emotional and legal worries. Hazel was really offended when the paralegal accused her of being a "mental case".

3. A FRIEND IN NEED

When Hazel decided to go to the welfare department she wanted some moral support and asked a friend to accompany her. The friend promised but was unavailable when Hazel was ready. The friend was either forgetful or irresponsible. She did not realize that Hazel was feeling very vulnerable that day, and that failing to provide Hazel with support could be a life altering experience that would push her closer to the breaking point. Hazel, who was already brokenhearted about her husband, her mother and the paralegal, was sensitive and raw. She was ready to crash. All her emotional supports were breaking down one by one.

4. UNPROFESSIONAL SOCIAL WORKER
Hazel's encounter with the insensitive social worker at the welfare office was the last straw. The social worker, hired to serve the community and be caring and compassionate to her clients, was judgmental. Rather than helping Hazel financially and emotionally, she gave her a lecture on internet relationships and made her feel awful about her long distance marriage. I once heard of a case in which a man who been treated insensitively and disrespectfully at the welfare office returned with a gun to kill someone and was arrested by the police. In Hazel's case she kept quiet and remained respectful to the social worker, but came home licking her wounds from another emotional trauma. The social worker did not realize that she was dealing with a suicidal woman who was barely holding on.

5. AN EMOTIONAL BOIL
When Hazel was hurt repeatedly in a short period of time, she felt hopeless and helpless. She had a painful moment of realization. She said, "I suddenly realized that my friend let me down, my kids were not there to help me, my mother was emotionally abusive and finally the welfare woman insulted me and I felt like an idiot. I felt like an emotional boil that was ready to burst." Many people who are not psychiatrists and psychologists wonder what a nervous breakdown is

like. Hazel's description of "an emotional boil that was ready to burst" is a very powerful way to describe it.

6. BIRTHDAY, A DAY TO DIE

I am always curious why people decide to choose a particular day to be the last day of their life. Human beings do not choose the day of their birth but they can choose the day of their death. Hazel chose that day as she was not sure that anyone would recognize her birthday. Had that happened, it would have been devastating and she did not want to face that possibility. That would have proven to her beyond any shadow of doubt that nobody cared. It was her worst fear. She said, "If they didn't, I didn't want to know and there just didn't seem any point to life." It is interesting to see that she used "didn't" three times in one sentence, reflecting her negative state of mind just before her final choice of suicide.

7. CHOOSING THE METHOD OF SUICIDE

Many men use violent means to kill themselves. Some use fire arms or jumping from a bridge or throwing themselves in front of a train. In Toronto, the Bloor Street Viaduct was so popular as a place to commit suicide that the city council opted to enclose it in mesh. Hazel, on the other hand, chose to use a sharp knife to slit her throat and bleed to death.

8. PLACE OF SUICIDE

Hazel did not want to kill herself at home as she did not want her family to have bad memories of her home. She told me in one of her sessions that she did not want her dogs licking her blood flowing out of her bedroom. I was amazed that even at the time of death Hazel was thoughtful about her family and her dogs. It reflected to me that although she was upset and hurt and disappointed by the behavior of her dear ones, at some deeper level she was still connected with them and considered them when deciding when and where to commit suicide. It was not an easy choice to make. It seemed as if she did not want to die, she just did not want to live, as living was becoming more painful than the idea of death. The German philosopher, Schopenhauer had said, 'When the horrors of living outweigh the horrors of dying, human beings commit suicide'. Hazel could not see any hope in living so she decided to end all her misery and pain, especially the pain of rejection from some of her dear ones.

9. WRITING LETTERS

I found it interesting that while she was contemplating suicide, she was emotionally connecting with her sister and children and her therapist by writing letters. That was the proof of her emotional bond with them. I was quite touched that she felt so connected with me that she wrote her last letter to me. She knew that I genuinely cared about her and wanted her to heal and start a new life after marriage. Hazel is a woman of integrity. I am impressed that before her death she wanted to pay the debt of $300 that she had borrowed from a friend. She shared that trait with Socrates, who after drinking a cup of hemlock, requested his disciple to pay his debt to a friend. Hazel, like Socrates, wanted to die with a clear conscience.

10. STRANGERS CARE

While Hazel suffered from a lack of care from some of her dear ones, she received caring and compassion from strangers. A couple of strangers helped her with booster cables and also a woman gave her a hug. That woman did not realize that a hug could make the difference of life and death for Hazel. She did not realize that she was extending emotional arms to a woman whose mother lacked them. In my opinion, that affectionate and caring hug of a stranger was significant in the turn of events in Hazel's life. That hug proved to Hazel that there are still people in this world who have a compassionate heart and who care for humanity. That woman knew the power of empathy. She knew and practiced the golden rule of doing unto others what you would like to be done to you.

11. EYE OF AN ARTIST

While Hazel was disconnecting with humans, she was still connecting with nature, animals and birds. She could see the beauty of loons, ducks and seagulls. Aesthetically she was offended by the ugliness of the diesel fumes. She did not want to die at a dirty beach or a filthy gas station. Hazel's aesthetic needs played a role in delaying her suicide. I always mentioned to Hazel that she was an artist and a writer and needed to write her life story that would inspire many people. Virginia Woolf was so particular about her writing style that she delayed her suicide for a few days as she wanted to create a perfect suicide note for her husband, Leonard Woolf. Hazel's writing style is impressive. Even her suicide notes are part of literature. Even her last line to her husband, "I wish that these were words of undying love instead of just 'dying'"… is a masterpiece. Even when she was dying, she was writing lines that could live forever in literature.

12. FEELING TIRED AND EXHAUSTED

After a sixteen hour struggle to find a lonely place and enough courage to kill herself, Hazel felt exhausted, realizing that she was a peaceful person and could not conjure enough violence to slit her throat. Hazel had not realized that suicide was not only a painful act but also a violent one. When she wrote to me, "Please do not think I took the easy way out. This is my bravest act yet." Hazel, even in her most vulnerable moments, did not want to come across as weak. That was her self image. All her life she was strong and powerful, like a rock. But when the rock was turning into sand she did not know how to cope. Even her friends and family members did not realize that she needed help. The woman who offered help to others all her life as a mother, daughter and a friend, did not know how to ask for help. She did not realize she was driving on an empty tank nor did she know how to fill it.

Many volunteers at Distress Centers are asked to keep a suicide caller engaged on the phone until the suicide urge leaves them. It is a common observation that a strong suicide urge, like any strong urge, is like a wave. People are acutely suicidal for a short period of time and then they lose the intensity of the urge. Hazel also got tired and for her the intensity decreased with time.

13. FAMILY WAITING

Hazel had no idea what to expect when she came back home after sixteen painful hours of driving and contemplating suicide. She was shocked to find her whole family waiting. When she had left she was afraid nobody would notice or recognize her, but when she returned she was welcomed by her sister's open arms. The presence of her sister's emotional arms to hug her was a symbolic replacement of her mother's arms that were absent.

14. POLICE AND HOSPITAL

Many relatives and friends struggle with the idea of calling the police. That is why when Amy called me, she was reluctant to call the police as she was afraid that she might offend Hazel. I reassured her and encouraged her to call the police as they had resources to find her and take her to the hospital. In my opinion when someone's life is in danger, we need to get all the help we can get to save their life.

15. DOCTOR WITH CLIPBOARD QUESTIONS

Hazel was very offended by the duty doctor in the emergency room who was asking her "clipboard questions". For him Hazel was Patient No. 33 for that evening in his 12 hour shift. He seemed to be insensitive to the needs of people with emotional problems. He did not realize that assessing someone with a broken leg is different than assessing someone with a broken heart.

16. COMPASSIONATE SOCIAL WORKER AND PSYCHIATRIST

Hazel was fortunate to have finally met a social worker who was kind and caring. She made Hazel feel important and special and expressed her compassion, quite the opposite of the social worker she had met in the welfare department.

When Hazel saw the psychiatrist, she was ready to accept his suggestions. That psychiatrist knew me and that made her feel comfortable. Her children staying in the hospital for a few hours also proved that they deeply cared for her.

17. FAMILY SUPPORT

Hazel's sister's stay for two weeks was the final confirmation of her family's support. They were willing to go out of their way to help her heal and recover. Hazel realized that she had misunderstood her family. Since they did not know how much she was hurting, they had not come forward to extend their help.

When I invited all the family members to our clinic for a family meeting, Hazel was pleasantly surprised that eight people showed up. Their presence alone proved a point. Hazel, who had been feeling so alone, started feeling re-connected with the loving bonds of her family members. Therapy helps people to correct their perceptions. Only genuine experiences change those perceptions. When Hazel experienced real care, concern and support from her family, she took another step towards healing.

18. A BREAKTHROUGH

Hazel is realizing that she can transform her breakdown into a breakthrough with some emotional help from her family and professional help from her therapist. I have seen a gradual improvement, healing and recovery in the last few weeks. She told me in the last session that she is recognizing that she is getting better as she has started to smile and laugh again. The last letter she wrote to me ended,

Laugh or Cry? This weekend I will choose to laugh. No other choice in the matter.
Laughingly yours
Hazel

I am worthy of the joyful and loving light that I freely and courageously share with you.

PART FIVE - AN AFFECTIONATE POEM FROM A LOVING SISTER

A few days later, I received a letter from Hazel's poet sister, Laura who stayed with Hazel for two weeks.

Dear Dr. Sohail,
Hazel has invited me to your book launching this Saturday and I am looking forward to it very much. Hazel is coming along and we have so much to be thankful for. First and foremost, I want to thank you for all the support and caring you have obviously given to my sister. I don't know what she would do without you in her life and having you for her doctor I have seen

*many over the years and you are
exceptional. I wish I could have seen you at
those times in my life. Anyway, I want to
wish you good luck on Saturday, may it be a
wonderful day for you. You are one of
Hazel's Angels, a very important one to say
the least. I wrote a poem about Angels. I
have enclosed it here for you.*

Take care and God Bless.

ANGELS AMONG US
*There are Angels among us
That we cannot see
Sent down from Heaven
To care for you and me*

*Everyone has a guardian Angel
To be by their side night and day
To walk with you each step you take
The right decisions they help you make*

*When you are sad and tears may fall
Your Angel helps to wipe them all
While counting each and every one
To be bottled in Heaven beyond the sun*

*Angels are anywhere and everywhere
In all human shapes and sizes
They do God's bidding without a care
And only a few even know they are there
So if you feel that no one cares
What you are going through
Remember your guardian Angel
Is right there beside you*

Dr. K. Sohail/Bette Davis

For God wants no one to be alone
His love he needs to share
While he reigns on his heavenly throne
He sends his Angels here.
Laura,
Hazel's oldest Sis xxxx

Being a secular humanist, it is not very often that I am called an angel. When I received the letter and the poem, I smiled and accepted the compliment as it was offered with love.

PART SIX - A BREAKTHROUGH WITH HER MOM - INTERVIEW WITH HAZEL

Sohail: *Thank you very much for agreeing to be interviewed again. It has been almost a year since we had our first interview when you went through a major crisis on your birthday last year. Fortunately you transformed your breakdown into a breakthrough. I am curious to know what was the major change that has taken place in the last year of your life?*

Hazel: In my first interview I had described my crisis as a boil that was ready to burst. It was an extremely painful experience. Afterwards, it was all but impossible to see my mother, or to speak to her or even to be around her even though she was living downstairs in my house. The tough part was that I was responsible for her care on a day to day basis. And soon afterwards she became more and more dependent on me for her care. Whenever I met with her she was full of complaints, gossiping and ridiculing others. She had no acknowledgment or appreciation for all the things I did for her and basically she had become even more bitter than she had in the past with no interest in life, love or living. I truly suffered being in her presence and there was quite literally no way out. I had to deal with her and my own disdain for her....I had to survive her and her situation as well as my own.

　　　　But then one day a transformation took place in me when I realized that she could not help who she was. I felt compassion for her. It was not love for my mother but basic human compassion. So I learned to let go of my expectations of her and I first began to pity her, rather than to chafe at her miserable personality. My pity then transformed into compassion for her as I realized that she was doing the best she could do. I also realized that she was locked down into who she was, and would never budge in her resolve to be her own person, as difficult as that was to fathom. I couldn't begin to comprehend her attitude, outlook or personality in relation to me or anyone else for that matter. She was her own person. Like it or lump it. Gradually I tapped into an old coping mechanism that I had with her when I was still a young child - I defied her orneriness with my humour. You would have to be familiar with the Irish sense of humour to fully appreciate what I mean. It's a "call a spade a spade" attitude with an honest openness that I suppose can only be appreciated by some. When I tapped into that humour, I was able to cope with her better and feel more compassion towards her. I thought it was the end of her life and she was literally going out of the door of life. It was a sad state of affairs. I thought she deserved some dignity and should leave this world on her own terms. Her greatest fear was to end up in a hospital or institution at the mercy of callous, incompetent doctors and staff. My mother made it difficult for anyone to care for her. Whenever I took her to see a doctor or a specialist she complained and bitched about it. She was very critical. It was also interesting that she complained to me far more than her other children. Gradually I realized that she harboured a lot of anger and resentment at life and I learned to detach from her emotionally. That was my saving grace.

Sohail: *Was her relationship with you different than her relationship with other siblings?*

Hazel: I think at the most fundamental level, her relationship with me was a little more honest than the relationship with my siblings. Especially at the end, in the last few months of her life, her health declined and there was just no getting around the fact, she was dying. The whistle was blown. Medical support workers were alerted to her condition and they stepped in to try to assist and govern her condition. In the beginning, she would not let them in as she thought they were invading her privacy and she baulked at them. I had to explain her personality to the various community workers that were coming in to *try* to assist her as she was very private and she simply would not cooperate with them. After a good attempt to aid her with Personal Support Workers, the organization gave up in the assistance department. A supervisor did come and complete a final analysis on her while confirming also with us, both that she was dying and wished to pass away at home, without medical intervention or assistance. My mother verbally acknowledged those facts and agreed with them.

During that time something changed inside me, not only for her but also for the rest of the family. It hit home with me that her life was ending. Her physical body was giving out and I was the only one here who seemed to give a care about her. My siblings were absent. She was my responsibility alone. She was having mini strokes that were incapacitating her body as well as her mind and the remarkable thing was that they were also chipping away at her cantankerous, bitter, angry nature.

My siblings had stopped visiting her some time before this. They rarely even telephoned her, despite emails from me reporting her declining health. As she began slipping away they still did not come. I found that to be incomprehensible. These children of hers had always put her on a pedestal and denied much of their ill feelings towards her for as long as I could remember and yet they would not come to see her or call her. Again, I could not fathom this. I remember how, in one of our sessions I told you how upset I was with them for neglecting her. I couldn't believe that they would stay away and how uncaring they all seemed and you told me, *"They can't"*. It took a while before that comment sunk in and then I realized that they could not even force themselves to be present with this woman who was their mother. And I accepted them for who they were. I realized they had their limitations and I let go of all the expectations I had from these people in my life. I felt great compassion for both my mother and for my siblings. That was a major change in me. I was our mother's sole caregiver - it was really that complicated and that simple.

Sohail: *So you became more accepting of the whole situation?*

Hazel: Yes. And it actually gave me strength because I realized I was doing more for my mother than she had ever done for me or my siblings. And that brought some peace for me. Not a sense of superiority, just peace.

Sohail: *So that was a major shift from the time when you needed a lot of support to the time when you offered a lot of support. You became a care taker and became very strong.*

Hazel: Super strong, stronger than ever.

Sohail: *Can you share the kind of relationship you had with your mom all your life, as a child, as a teenager and as an adult?*

Hazel: My relationship with my mom was always different than the relationship she had with my siblings. As far as I remember she was always extremely harsh and short tempered and irritable. She was always very, very stressed and took it out on us. There was so much tension in our house you could cut it with a knife. And then I realized one day that there was an elephant in the room but nobody was willing to talk about it. So I started to challenge my mother as I realized we did not have to live with that drama and trauma. We did not have to put up with her harsh treatment. That changed our relationship. There were times there would be an awkward silence and then we would laugh. I was more honest with her than her other children as I could no longer pretend.

Sohail: *What happened that she started living with you rather than the other children?*

Hazel: Well for years my siblings, particularly my two sisters, would rant about my mother being in Toronto on her own in her apartment and her health was failing. But my mother wanted to be independent and determined. She acted like a martyr. All my siblings complained but none of them offered her to come and live with them. So I decided to get a house in which there was an apartment for her and she moved with me.

Sohail: *For how long did she live with you?*
Hazel: She lived with me since the year 2000, for eleven years. She was already 85 years old at that time when she moved in. She was 96 when she passed on.

Sohail: *What was the date when she passed on?*
Hazel: March 23, 2011

Sohail: *That was pretty close to your birthday again.*
Hazel: Yes

Sohail: *Tell me about the last few weeks of her life. What happened?*
Hazel: In the last few weeks of her life she had a series of stokes. She had a major stoke at a restaurant but then came out of it and refused to go to the hospital. She was in total denial. She became very fragile and finally let her guard down. In the last few weeks she became humble and accepting of her life condition. When I took over her care I cooked all her meals and did all the shopping for her. She tried to maintain her pride and I used my sense of humour.

Sohail: *So how did the story end? What happened at the end?*

Hazel: Some visitors were supposed to come to see her but she was very, very weak and I knew it was the end. I went downstairs and she was still asleep and that made me suspicious because she got up same time very early every morning. She used to get up, get dressed, make her breakfast - she had a routine. Even when she was sick and dying of pneumonia, she still got up and got dressed and made her bed, read her newspaper and did her crossword puzzles. So when I saw her in bed I realized there was something wrong. I put the kettle on the stove hoping that she would get up. Later on I realized she had a stroke through the night and did not remember much. She wanted to sleep on the couch that was very unusual for her. I left the night light on in the hall. The following morning when I went down I found her sleeping on the couch fully dressed. Her eyes were open and she was gasping for breath. I realized that she had another stroke while sleeping on the couch. So I called 911 and tried CPR as she was gasping. The ambulance came and took her to the hospital. She survived for two more days in the hospital. The second day she was there she was in deep coma. At 5 in the morning when all of us were there, her breathing changed. Two of my sisters were asleep. I woke them up. We all stood around the bed and she took a few more breaths and then she was gone. And I thought, "She was gone without saying anything to her children". She shared nothing, she did not connect with us at all.

Sohail: *It has been a few weeks now since she passed away. How do you feel about all that now?*

Hazel: I feel good as I did all I could do for her. I forgave that horrible monster and I found some compassion for her in my heart. Finally, just before she died, I had a breakthrough with her that I did not have all of our lives. I feel proud of myself for doing that.

Sohail: *Thank you for sharing your story.*
Hazel: You are quite welcome.

PART SEVEN - CONCLUDING COMMENTS

I feel fortunate that as a psychotherapist I can help my patients transform their breakdowns into breakthroughs. I feel lucky to know Hazel. I am impressed by her loving nature and inspired by her resilience.

Hazel's story tells all of us - whether friends or family members, professionals or lay people - how human relationships can make or break people. Some professionals or friends who speak or act insensitively can push people over the edge, while strangers with a caring comment or an affectionate hug can help a suicidal person choose life over death. Life is full of surprises and mysteries, and some stories are more mysterious than others.

Note...I would like to thank Hazel and Laura for being generous enough to give me permission to include their letters, interview and poem in my essay, hoping that it would help other patients and their dear ones to light a candle of hope in their darkest hours. I have changed the names of people to respect their privacy.

Chapter Four

Creating an Emotional First Aid Kit
- Interview with Mary Ann

Sohail: *Mary Ann, thank you very much for agreeing to be interviewed for this project. I think you have some special ideas and experiences that will help many other people. I am aware you went through a very serious breakdown. Can you share what happened that painful night?*

Mary Ann: It was October 1st 2009, a day to be remembered. During the day I went for a biopsy at the hospital. They tried many times but were unsuccessful. I had no pain throughout the day but I had great pain in the evening. The pain accompanied by the frustration of not being able to sleep, the anxiety of a business gone bankrupt and the loneliness of a daughter in Vancouver, that day it all culminated. It came to me for one brief moment in time that there was no hope. This was not a planned attempt. It was a moment in time where you are in a corner, a nano-second, in the time it takes to blink, there was no hope. Even as a Jesus follower who believes that there's hope for all eternity, there wasn't any. I succeeded at that time to take 285 tablets because I just wanted to go to sleep. I didn't want to kill myself, I didn't want to be dead, I just wanted to go to sleep. When I woke up I thought I had a weird dream, I usually don't remember my dreams. I got up to go to the bathroom and I started to throw up. At that time I realized it wasn't a dream, it was real. I threw up and I threw up. I woke my husband up who had been sleeping and told him, "Darling I have done the most foolish thing, I need to go to the hospital. Please call the ambulance." That was the beginning of my hospitalization for detoxification, getting on the right meds and starting to recover.

Sohail: *Was that the first time you had taken an overdose or thought of ending your life?*
Mary Ann: I wouldn't say it was the first time I thought of suicide. I had dark and sinister thoughts in the past. I had thought about how I would end my life but I was too scared to do it.

Sohail: *I remember the time when another psychiatrist told you that you suffered from Bipolar Disorder. Can you share how you felt after hearing your diagnosis?*
Mary Ann: That was horrible time, it went on for months. I couldn't even think about it because it upset me so much. I believed the lie that I was defective and mentally deranged. It was more than upsetting. It made me feel physically sick to think about that.

Sohail: *How did your hospitalization affect your family members?*
Mary Ann: It affected them in various manners. My husband was just beside himself with anxiety. He is an anxious person anyway but he had that shallow breathing and wide-eyed glossy look when he would come into the hospital to see me because he was so

frightened. My daughter's reaction was that of anger even though she was out in Vancouver.

Sohail: *Was that your daughter who said, "How can you be so selfish"?*
Mary Ann: Yes. How could I be so selfish? How could I do this to the family especially my husband, their dad? Funny enough I had always believed myself that the most selfish thing that anybody could do was to commit suicide and there I was myself attempting it. Looking back now I realize that one cannot make assumptions like that. You cannot make blanket statement like that because you never ever know what's going on in someone else's head.

Sohail: *And your son?*
Mary Ann: My son was away at university. He is my husband's best friend. Brett and his dad got closer through that but I don't really know how that affected him. After the episode he went to purchase an engagement ring. He said that the defining moment when he knew that his girlfriend, was for him was when he called her and said, "my mom's in the hospital, she's sick." She did not brush him off. She accepted him and let him share what was going on in his life. Jess was concerned about his family life and that clinched in his mind that she was the right person for him. So something beautiful came out of something horrible.

Sohail: *In your mind what helped you to feel better?*
Mary Ann: Well, number one was God's grace. Number two were all the people that were put in my path. The psychiatrist at the hospital went from one

facility to another by ambulance with me. He saw my medications and suggested that they needed to be changed. Paramedics were also very caring and concerned and the staff in the hospital was very supportive. They kept me in the hospital until I was accepted in the Mental Health Day Hospital. After I was discharged from Day Hospital I came back to your group in Creative Psychotherapy Clinic.

Sohail: *What did you feel about the family meeting we had when your daughter was visiting from Vancouver? Did that help?*
Mary Ann: I think it brought the issues to the surface. I realized that some thing as serious as this couldn't be swept under the rug. In our family nobody knew how to talk about the elephant in the room. Your family meeting helped us address those issues. You were the third party facilitating the process. It was very helpful. We realized how much we need each other as a couple and as a family. My daughter had a chance to express her anger.

Sohail: *How do you feel now out of ten?*
Mary Ann: If I was zero the day I attempted suicide, I am 8 now.

Sohail: *Roughly how much time have passed since that happened?*
Mary Ann: It started in October and now it's May.

Sohail: *So it's about 6 months?*
Mary Ann: Yes, and it is unbelievable.

Sohail: *During this time you mentioned creating an Emotional First Aid Kit to help yourself if you are ever in a crisis or a difficult situation like this in the future. I found that concept very helpful and I want others to benefit and to adopt that concept of self-support. Can you share what is in your Emotional First Aid Kit?*

Mary Ann: Yes, I do strongly, strongly suggest that everyone who has serious emotional issues need to create an Emotional First Aid Kit. I have a little box, kept in a safe place, in which I keep the following:

1. Emergency medications from my psychiatrist
2. Phone numbers of my psychiatrist and your clinic
3. 911 to call an ambulance
4. Phone numbers of three friends that I can call if I need help right away
5. Letters from people who are supportive and value me and told me what I mean to them.
6. A note that says that, this will pass and I will get better.
7. I also have a squeeze toy that helps me in decreasing my stress level.

Every person can make his or her own first aid kit and add things that would be helpful at the time of crisis.

Sohail: *You have transformed a breakdown into a breakthrough. How did that experience change you as a person?*

Mary Ann: I feel as if I have taken off the dirty coat of shame and stigma. I feel as if I have a new beginning, starting a new life. I have so much to be grateful for, so much to be thankful for. I have accepted that I suffer from Bipolar Disorder and I have to take medications maybe for the rest of my life, maybe not. I accept my condition and will try my best to stay healthy. I certainly did not plan on a suicide attempt. If you were to say to me 20 years ago, "Mary Ann, when you are 50 years old, you are going to have a suicide attempt." I would have said, "Get out, don't be silly." But it happened.

Sohail: *Now you are back to work?*
Mary Ann: Yes, I'm back to work and it's funny because as progressive as we think we are in 2010, you still get people that are back in the Stone Age. One person that I work with said, "Oh I thought it was all in your head". Now I realize that mental health issues aren't just in your head they are total body experiences. So you do get the idiots who are ignorant.

Sohail: *And you are back socializing with your friends?*
Mary Ann: Yes, I had always kept in touch with people, my circle of great friends. There's one friend in particular who called me every day. I know she found it very difficult to do as her mother committed suicide and she found her. For her to do that, to call me every day, that was really hard but she did.

Sohail: *I am glad you have a caring family and supportive friends. You are fortunate to have a supportive network that helped you recover and heal and grow. Our grouptherapy members feel very connected to you and missed you when you were in the hospital. They are happy to see you alive and well.*

LETTER TO MARY ANN - WISDOM OF THE HEART

Dear Mary Ann,

In our last session I was quite pleased to see your mood chart reflecting your progress, highlighting that you have been emotionally stable for the last six months. You have worked very hard in therapy and your story is a great inspiration for many in our group. You are a kind, caring and compassionate person. I am impressed by the generosity of your spirit. I remember the time when you were emotionally vulnerable and going through a roller coaster ride. I remember the time when you were haunted by your painful past, the troubling nightmare of your childhood that undermined your self esteem.

You are lucky to have created a supportive family. Meeting your husband and daughter in a family therapy session after your suicide attempt provided me with an opportunity to reassure them, answer their questions and share with them that your suicide attempt was accidental, reflecting your sense of desperation and temporary hopelessness. There was no intention to hurt anyone, especially your loving family. Talking to a therapist did reassure your daughter and helped build a bridge of compassion between the two of you.

It was so wonderful to meet your son last month, who is in love and enjoying life. I was so impressed by the loving card he gave you on your last birthday.

I am quite aware that it was very hard for you to cope when your other doctor diagnosed you with Bipolar Disorder and ordered mood stabilizers. I am quite pleased that you have accepted it and with the help of medications and psychotherapy, you are able to control the symptoms. You are aware now that suffering from Depression is neither a crime nor a sin. You have no reason to be ashamed or embarrassed. There were many writers, scholars and philosophers in history, who suffered from Depression. Bipolar Disorder seems to have great affinity with creativity and you are quite a creative person.

I am pleased to see that you have gone back to work to serve your community as well as your family.

Your concept and creation of the Emotional First Aid Kit is invaluable. I have shared that concept with many of my other patients and they found it quite useful. I hope one day your concept is included in psychiatric text books and self help programs as it has great potential to help many people who suffer from serious emotional problems and mental illness. It is your brilliant gift to humanity.

Your story is a great source of inspiration. I feel honored to be your therapist. I have learnt many things from you. You have the wisdom of the heart.

Sincerely,
Sohail
July 17th, 2010

Dr. K. Sohail/Bette Davis

Chapter Five

I Will Fly
- Jamie L. Millen

Looking down at the droplets of blood on the sand, I wondered how I had gotten to this point. The pain in my soul screamed to cut harder, but my mind filled with images of my family - my husband, my mom and dad, and my in-laws. How could I do this to them? The damaged part of me argued that they would all be better off with me gone. I gript the razor blade tighter and held it to my wrist. In my heart I knew that my death would devastate them. I looked at the blade. It was too dull to do the job. My choices were clear – go get another one or go get help.

I sat down in the sand and pressed a few tissues to my wrist. I refused to call my psychiatrist. The woman had let me walk out of her office that morning in spite of my insistence that she would not see me again - the threat of suicide was very clear. The truth was that in the three years that I had been her patient, all she had succeeded in doing was drug me half-out of my mind. I got up, brushed the sand off and headed for my car.

The drive to the walk-in clinic where my doctor worked was quick. Before I knew it, she had cleaned the cuts on my wrists and offered me two choices: to return to the hospital where my psychiatrist worked or be in a locked ward at a psychiatric hospital. I opted for the locked ward. Her assistant took me to the local hospital for medical clearance before I was transferred to the psychiatric hospital.

When the door locked behind me, every nerve in my body tensed. *"Run!"* my mind screamed. I had been on a regular psychiatric ward twice before in a medical hospital, but never on a locked ward in a psychiatric facility. It freaked me out. The nurse guided me into a small storage room. She explained that it was necessary for her to search me for my safety and others on the ward. As her hands patted down my pockets, my mind fled back to the beach. I was now seriously regretting my choice.

Adjusting to life on the ward took some time. At first I was in a private room which kept me on my guard at night. I was scared that a male patient might enter into my room. I slept better once I was moved into the female dorm. Even though I was safe surrounded by others, I still didn't feel safe from myself. The urge to hurt myself was still strong.

The nurse that was assigned to me was a no-nonsense person who realized that I was still a danger to myself. She sat me down one day and told me that if I didn't change my behaviour, everyone I loved would be forced to leave me because they could not watch me destroy myself. She said that she had seen this happen to other patients. I thought about what it would be like to watch my husband, my parents and my in-laws all turn away from me to preserve their own sanity. I realized how much my behaviour must hurt them. I admitted to her that I didn't really want to die; I just wanted the pain to stop. She said that there was a solution; a nine-month in - hospital program that had excellent results. The only catch was I had to promise to not hurt myself or I would not be accepted into the program.

That afternoon as I curled up on my bed and thought about starting another in-hospital program, my mood started to drop fast. Depression is like a black blanket that wraps itself around you so tight that you can't breathe, can't see, can only feel its embrace and it's the only thing you can think about. I felt its hold tightening on me. I just wanted to escape. I had wanted to escape for a long time. I was 27 and had battled thoughts of suicide since I was about 16 years old. I tried to figure what had caused the blackness within me, but there was no specific incident or reason that I could pin point as the cause. It was just there. An unwanted part of me; growing in intensity and duration. Weekly shrink sessions, psychiatric meds, even a stint in day treatment had not lessened the depression. Now I was locked up and again I was faced with two choices: continue on this path of self-destruction until I succeeded in killing myself or enter this new program and work it because my life depended on it.

I got up and started pacing the room; looking for anything that I could use to hurt myself. My nurse walked in and tried to calm me down.

"I know you're hurting," she said softly.

"I just want to die. I don't even know why," I cried. "Why don't you just let me die?"

"Once you get out of here, I can't stop you. But I can't help you if you're dead. Let me help you."

"I guess a corpse makes a lousy patient," I quipped through my tears.

From Breakdowns to Breakthroughs

The nurse smiled at me. "The worst. So are you going to let us help you?"

I spent nine months in the in-patient unit. It was a specialized program that focused on intensive psychotherapy without the use of medication and encouraged the patient to be accountable for their actions and in their treatment. The program required me to live on the unit during the week and permitted me to return home on the weekends. It was difficult for my husband and me, but it was necessary. We both realized that it might be my only chance to turn my life around.

After about two months in the program, the first piece of my life-long puzzle, as to why I was depressed, fell into place. I had my first flashback. At the time, the nurses did not label it a flashback; instead they took a wait-and-see approach. However, a very detailed flashback the following month confirmed their suspicions- I had been sexually abused as a child. In the flashback, I saw his face, what he was doing to my small-child's body and where the incident took place. The revelation left me reeling. More flashbacks and body memories followed. I felt more depressed and suicidal than ever before. With the caring support of my therapists, I survived the memories. They cared about me, and they got me to care about myself. The most important lesson they taught me was that I mattered and I was worth fighting for.

After I left the program, I joined two weekly therapy groups, both for sexual abuse survivors, and sought out a new therapist for weekly sessions. The A.M.A.C. (Adults Molested As Children) group was brutal, but I went because I desperately needed the support to endure all of the new memories that were bombarding me. I still felt suicidal most of the time, but clung to the belief that I shouldn't have to die because of what my abuser did to me. I deserved to live. I mattered, and even if I didn't believe that in the moment, I knew that my family and the therapists I worked with on the unit believed that. I held on.

Two years out of the program, I made the most important decision of my life. My husband and I wanted to have children, but before I could do that, I had to promise myself that suicide would never again be an option for me. I owed it to my future children that they would have a mother who would be there for them and would never leave them by choice. Nine months later my precious daughter was born, followed two years later by my precious son. I'm blessed to have them in my life.

My children make everything clear for me. I have to take care of myself in order to be able to take care of them. I took a few years off from therapy when the kids were toddlers. When my youngest started nursery school, I started to feel depressed again. Worried that it would spiral out of control, I decided to go back into therapy and looked for a new therapist.

The search was daunting. One therapist fell asleep during our second session. Another yelled at me because she wanted me to pay more money than I could afford. Another almost doubled her rates after a year, making it impossible for me to afford therapy with her. Another was inexperienced and did not know how to handle my suicidal feelings even though I promised not to act on them. I had learned a long time ago that I would still have those feelings at times, but I didn't have to act on them.

After several false starts, I was finally referred to Dr. Sohail and the Creative Psychotherapy Clinic by my family physician. Since I had never worked primarily with a male therapist before, I didn't know if I would be able to get past my abuse issues and be able to trust him and connect with him. I decided to try. Fortunately for me, Dr. Sohail was really smart and didn't try to force a connection. Instead he built up a rapport with me using a mutual interest - writing. He asked me to bring in a copy of the memoir that I was writing and share it with him. Getting another writer's opinion on my work was irresistible to me, so for the next several months, I spent each session reading the chapter that I had written that week. I often brought in poems that I wrote too. Through my writing, he got to know me on a very deep level. And I got to trust him, first as a fellow writer, then as my therapist.

Time has gone by quickly. My kids are teenagers. I'm still in therapy with Dr. Sohail who now knows me way better than I know myself. Depression is still a problem, but I can handle it. I've learned to accept that I will feel depressed at times and I no longer berate myself for it, but try to take care of myself instead. I've accepted that the depression is the long-term effect of the abuse. At times I still have suicidal feelings, but I now realize that those feelings will pass. I just have to wait it out. I also know enough now to reach out for help before things spiral out of control. I also trust Dr. Sohail to protect me from myself if necessary. Therapy can be very painful and difficult, but also very rewarding. I know that I've grown and changed for the better because of it. Therapy has given me back my life.

I WILL FLY

Take another drink
Hit another wall
Without their love
I'm nothing at all.
Pop another pill
Smash another glass
Without their love
I'd drown in my past.
Yell another curse
Pound another nail
Without their love
I'd surely fail.

Fake another smile
Stifle another cry
Without their love
I'd never get by.

Dry another tear
Brave another day
Without their love
There would be no way.

Take another step
Give another try
With their love
I will fly.

Chapter Six

Seeing Women as Friends - Interview with Robert

Sohail: *Thank you for agreeing to share your story of emotional suffering and healing in therapy. What do you remember of the time when you first came to see me?*
Robert: I remember I was at a loss. I really didn't know what options I had. I felt as if life was closing in on me and it was scary.

Sohail: *What were the areas in your life that you were unsure about?*
Robert: I was unsure about my relationships. I was unsure about myself particularly in regards to my sexuality and my acting out. Those were the two big areas I really didn't know how to deal with. I had lost control. I had no sense of self control.

Sohail: *What do you remember of the journey spiraling down hill?*
Robert: I remember episodes of extreme anxiety and particularly later on, I can remember the anxiety being so overwhelming and powerful that I actually thought I was going to black out. I thought I was going to lose my body functions. I would be in the hallway of my clinic, going from one adjusting room to another and worrying that I would lose my bowel and bladder

control. It was just a bad situation. I used to excuse myself from my patients and go out and go around the corner and get some fresh air to get my wits about me, and then come back in and treat another patient. I thought I was losing it.

Sohail: *Your breakdown coincided with you leaving Annette. How did that happen?*
Robert: I had known Annette since 1995. I had met her when I was temporarily separated from my wife and we got along very well when we first met each other. I went back to my wife, to see if I could re-create that same intimacy, but when the marriage started to deteriorate and Terri's drinking got even worse, I blamed myself. I could not leave her and be on my own, so I chose Annette and jumped ship. But that did not work either and I had a breakdown several years later.

Sohail: *Whose idea was it to come and see me?*
Robert: I had been involved with Al Anon, and my sponsor had seen you and highly recommended you, so I called and was on a waiting list for two years. This was when I was living with Annette after I had already left the marriage and I was still getting severe anxiety attacks with the divorce proceedings. When I had checked myself into the Ajax hospital, I saw Dr. Arfai and told him that I was giving up, that I was "throwing in the towel." He recommended that I continue to see you for my psychotherapy to help me. I just could not function. I could not even drive so my friend, Betty drove me for my appointment.

Sohail: *Were you worried that you might be hospitalized?*

Robert: Yes, I was expecting it.

Sohail: *And then what happened?*
Robert: I was in such a severe state of anxiety and paranoia, that Dr. Arfai felt I could not handle hospitalization because the psych ward was a lock-up facility, and he thought I would freak out and become psychotic. Another thing that struck me odd at the time was that he described me as narcissistic (laughs), which really threw me off. I could not believe that he would think of me as a narcissistic person, because with my own misperceptions of myself at the time, I really couldn't see myself realistically at all.

Sohail: *I remember suggesting to you to stay with your friends Betty and Daniel, rather than going to the hospital. How long did you stay there?*
Robert: For a full year.

Sohail: *So what was that year like for you?*
Robert: Most of the time I remember feeling quite defeated. I had the idea that I would bounce back quickly. I used to be anxious and impatient, but because of their life style being so much calmer, it just kind of kept the lid on things. Of course, they had me involved in day to day activities and chores around the house and things like that. For me to sit there would have driven me crazy and I felt safe there. I felt like a little kid, completely dependent on his parents.

Sohail: *So you felt like they were your surrogate parents?*
Robert: Yes.

Sohail: *When did you feel that you were starting to become better? What were the early signs of recovery?*
Robert: I think one of the first signs of recovery was that I wanted to e-mail. So I got a computer that was set up at their place and sent an email.

Sohail: *Were there times that you felt you would never get better?*
Robert: Yes, unfortunately.

Sohail: *Did you every think of ending your life?*
Robert: Many, many times.

Sohail: *Any plans, any attempts?*
Robert: No, no plans or attempts. I was just entertaining my thoughts of it. It happened to be invariably, if I would engross myself into starting to think about it, that the image of my son and my daughter would come to me, and I would think about the suffering, disgrace, and stigma they would have to face in their life if I did kill myself. That seemed to work and terminate the fantasy of suicide. I had a dramatic fantasy though. I fantasized of driving a knife straight through the heart. I did not like the idea or want to swallow drugs and be taken to the hospital and my stomach being pumped out. My love for my children kept me from committing suicide. I had met people whose parents had committed suicide and I did not want my children to deal with that. They were already dealing with a very nasty divorce

Sohail: *What were the factors that helped in your healing, recovery and rehabilitation?*

Robert: Well definitely staying with Daniel and Betty and my individual sessions with you. I also had unofficial sessions with my chiropractor friend, Dr. Knight. It would be at least once a week. He insisted that I would go there and sit with him and sometimes there wasn't a lot of discussion, but it was him checking in with me. He cared for and about me. That was a big factor. I also ended up spending a couple of weeks at home with my parents which I needed to do. I don't, even to this day, know what was the healing factor there, other than I think it was that they would accept me in the shape I was in. I think they needed to be a witness to my state of incapacity. It was a real issue to me that they accept me just as I was. I considered myself a complete and personal failure, so for my parents to spend time with me and accept the situation, was helpful.

Sohail: *Was that the first time you were involved in psychotherapy or did you have therapy before?*
Robert: No, I had some marital therapy before.

Sohail: *How was the experience with our clinic different than what you had experienced before or what you expected?*
Robert: Therapy with you helped me not only to talk, but also think and process. I did not do that in the past. I learned the process of thinking and contemplating and meditating. It was quite helpful. I learned to reflect on things you said. I learned to participate in my own healing and growth.

Sohail: *More active than passive.*
Robert: Yes.

Sohail: *And how was the combination of individual and group therapy work for you?*
Robert: Well, with the group I get to see the perspective of other people and their circumstances and I'm able to see and get a perspective of where I fit into the scheme of life. In other words, I learned that by helping others I can help myself. Rather than being self-centered and narcissistic, I can be empathic and selfless. Group therapy provides a good balance between the work within and the work without.

Sohail: *How did you decide to go back to work and start your practice again?*
Robert: I had no choice (laughing). When the insurance company cut off the money, that's when you recommended that I start attending my clinic for merely one or two hours a day. In the beginning it was a horrifying experience to just being there, let alone doing anything, or actually seeing patients. I wasn't sure how I could help my patients and children if I could not help myself. I was such a mess.

Sohail: *And how did you decide to leave Daniel and Betty and start living on your own?*
Robert: That was after I took that week long workshop called The Hoffman Process, where I came out from a depressed state straight into a hypomanic state of euphoria, and I think it was that energy of exhilaration that gave me this idea that, 'wow, there's a possibility and actually some hope for me, that I could live on my own'. So probably it was that hypo-manic state that gave me the courage and confidence. A total illusion! Although after that hypo-manic state

I did fall back into discouragingly depressive states a couple of times over the next two years.

Sohail: *Did medications contribute to managing your hypo-manic state?*
Robert: For a while I felt like a guinea pig trying different medications.

Sohail: *You don't think they helped you stabilize?*
Robert: Not that much.

Sohail: *So after moving on your own and heading back to work, how did you connect socially with your colleagues and friends?*
Robert: Well, I can't say that I have totally reconnected with friends and colleagues like I used to. I think it just started slowly with a few friends that made a point of checking in on me. Most of the social life that I'd had in the past, I no longer have. My lifestyle has changed after the recovery.

Sohail: *When did you feel that your breakdown could be transformed into a breakthrough?*
Robert: Probably about, I would say 4 years ago, and it had to do with Christine, a previous reliable, trustworthy, understanding, supportive and compassionate employee of mine, coming back into my life and my office. For me it was like a sign from God! It was a sign that my luck had changed, and that I had fought a good fight, and that I had gained favor with the gods so to speak, and that her arrival was a sign of that good favor. That inside of me, my worth had been manifested in good fortune.

Something good was finally going my way. That was about 4 years ago, maybe 5 years ago now.

Sohail: *How did you feel when you met Shelly and started an intimate relationship?*
Robert: I have been dating Barbara. I remember the time when I had just left the relationship with her. With Barbara, I had the idea that I could create a healthy relationship, but I ended on my butt once again. I was disappointed about that. With Shelly, first of all, we had our profession in common. We understood each other in the world of the professional and business life and we also had the factor of a large geographical distance to buffer our interactions and slow the momentum of our relationship. Our relationship started basically by e-mailing back and forth for months before we even started talking on the phone. I think it was the distance factor and very slow pace that allowed me to better process our interactions, and surprisingly enough, it actually kept my interest and attention alive enough to develop meaningfully.

Sohail: *How was that relationship different than your previous relationships?*
Robert: Well first of all, it was less impulsive; it was a relationship that gave me time to think about things instead of just acting impulsively on my wishes

Sohail: *Where is the relationship now?*
Robert: It was better this weekend than ever. I mean it's definitely growing.

Sohail: *You think it's better than your previous relationships?*
Robert: It's better than any relationship I have ever been in.

Sohail: *Has this relationship changed your attitude towards women?*
Robert: Of course. I think it taught me to respect a woman as a person firstly. It has taught me appreciation, and it has taught me gratitude. It has taught me what **love** is.

Sohail: *So there was a time when you were not monogamous?*
Robert: I could call my entire adolescent and adult relationship life "non-monogamous."

Sohail: *How do you deal with that aspect of your personality now?*
Robert: I still have a lot of thoughts about not being monogamous and faithful but then my thinking process kicks in and says, 'I don't think being unfaithful has greater value than keeping what I have right now. It's not worth losing what I have.' So I think I value our relationship more than any other one I've had in the past.

Sohail: *How has your relationship changed with your children?*
Robert: I think I'm learning how to accept them as people, instead of belongings.

Sohail: *Your son talks very affectionately about you.*

Robert: He's got my car for the night...he better be talking affectionately (Laughing). I'm glad that he sees me in that dimension now, that's for sure. That's really good. We are becoming friends.

Sohail: *What do you like most about yourself?*
Robert: I think I am a caring person. I'm really a genuine person. I really care for others.

Sohail: *And your sense of failure that you had?*
Robert: I can't say that I don't have a sense of failure at all, but many times I see that the failure that I have had in the past is something that was necessary for me to get me to where I am today. It was like a spring board. If I haven't had those failures, then I would be going though the same cycles.

So for some of those failures I can say that I've came to a point of being grateful for those failures. Yet for some other failures, I still have to get to the point of finding gratitude for them.

Sohail: *When you look at the future now what kind of a feeling do you have?*
Robert: I have a feeling of guarded promise. In other words, there's a sense of promise for the future for me, and at the same time I know I have to guard that promise well. That is where the metaphor of the turtle comes true for me. Slow and steady wins the race.

Sohail: *Is there any fear still about your future?*
Robert: Sure. I have a fear that I will fall back into old habits. I have a fear that I may not have the capacity to have a long term success. That this might be just an

uphill phase to a downhill journey so to speak. So yes, I do have fear about my future.

Sohail: *Looking back now on therapy, what were you expecting and what did you learn?*
Robert: I think that therapy taught me that I was the one that had to and needed to do the work. Therapy has been a very stabilizing experience for me. Let's put it this way: it's one of those things that to this very day, when it comes to Thursdays, I know if I've had a rough time or am going through some tough challenges, I know that if nothing else, I'm going to be in a safe place, and I will be able to get myself grounded again and see a different perspective. Thursdays are my therapy days for both my individual and group sessions. Now, I look forward to them, before I would dread them.

Sohail: *Any surprises in therapy that you did not expect?*
Robert: A couple of surprises. One is that it's taking a lot longer than I would ever think and yet, it's been more enjoyable than I ever thought. Secondly, I learned more about me and about other people than I ever thought possible.

Sohail: *So for those people who are reluctant to see a therapist, what would be your suggestion for them?*
Robert: Well, first of all I would say, interview a few therapists and choose the one that really cares about you and what you are going through. I am impressed by the compassion from which you work. I think that makes a big difference in the whole approach. It makes a huge difference in the dynamics and success of therapy.

Sohail: *How do you feel Bette and I worked together as co-therapists with you and Shelly and the group? What do you feel about that whole experience?*

Robert: I think it is great because typically speaking, we all are dealing with some kind of "mother" and "father" issues and by therapeutically playing out those roles within a healthy model, it makes it just perfect in creating a balanced experience. It is probably twice as effective as a single therapist perspective.

Sohail: *Any suggestions for those men who still see women as sex objects.*

Robert: I think it would be about inviting them to first discover and accept the feminine aspects of themselves and then being willing to see women as friends.

LETTER TO ROBERT - A SOURCE OF INSPIRATION

Dear Robert,

Thank you for sharing your story of healing and growth. As I was reading your interview I was reflecting on the milestones you achieved in the last few years. I am quite impressed by the changes you have made in therapy. I am quite aware that it was not easy for you but I hope you feel it was all worthwhile. You have transformed right in front of my eyes and I feel honored to be part of that process.

I remember when you were first referred by Dr. Arfai for psychotherapy. You were so distressed that your anxiety was paralyzing for you. You could not function and you could not look after yourself. I did not want to admit you to hospital so I suggested that you live with your friends, Betty and Daniel, who deeply cared for you. I was pleased and relieved that they accepted the challenge and became your surrogate parents for a year, the time you needed to recover from your emotional breakdown. It was the time a healer needed to heal.

I was quite touched to read in your interview that in spite of having suicidal thoughts you did not act on those thoughts as you did not want your children to deal with their father's suicide. I think that is one form of expression of your love for your children. I hope you have told them that they were a significant factor in your choosing life over death.

I think you were lucky to have friends like Betty, Daniel and Dr. Knight who offered you ongoing support and became your family of the heart.

After your recovery I was pleased that you could go back to work and gradually you could work more hours, reflecting your growth and recovery.

I was aware that you had difficult relationships with women. In your life your creativity, insanity and sexuality had become intimately connected. As you recovered, you had a chance to review your life in individual and group therapy. I was quite pleased when you started dating Shelly, not only because she belonged to the same profession, but also that she lived far away. I think if she lived in the same town, you might not been able to handle too much intimacy too soon. A long distance relationship provided you with time and space to heal and create a healthy intimate relationship.

I think it was helpful for both of you to see me and Bette, so that you could receive feedback from both of us. I think your relationship with Shelly helped you establish a healthy romantic relationship. I was impressed to see that you treated her with respect and became friends. For you to see women as friends first, rather than seeing them as sex objects, has been a breakthrough. I think you have come a long way since your breakdown. In some ways you seem more mature and wiser than ever before.

I was also pleased to see you working hard to have a healthy relationship with your children. Since I have talked to both of them, I am pleased that they have worked out their issues with you and now they can enjoy a healthy and loving relationship with you. It is better late than never. Now they know that you have always loved them. They did suffer as children because of your painful divorce. Now they are adults and they can establish an adult to adult affectionate relationship with you.

I think your involvement with group therapy was quite therapeutic for you. You had an opportunity to give and receive meaningful feedback. I am quite aware that your story has been a source of inspiration for many. Thanks for sharing your story and inspiring others. I learnt so much from you, your struggles and your triumphs.

Sincerely,
Sohail
July 22nd, 2010

Part Two

Green Zone Therapy

Chapter Seven

Green Zone Therapy

Over the decades I have realized that there are so many people all around us who silently suffer all their lives and not even their close friends and family members know the intensity of their emotional pain. It is partly because there is so much social stigma against mental illness that many people suffering from emotional problems feel ashamed and embarrassed to share their troubles with others. It is easier for people to publicly acknowledge that they suffer from physical problems, whether hypertension or diabetes, cirrhosis or cancer and others are sympathetic, but it is very difficult for people to acknowledge to others that they suffer from anxiety or depression, schizophrenia or bipolar disorder, marital problems or addictions because they are afraid that people will judge them and then ostracize them. It's sad that many never get professional or social help and suffer in silence.

After working in psychiatric hospitals, general hospitals and mental health clinics for years, I chose to start a psychotherapy clinic to develop a self-help program for my patients and their families. I wanted people with emotional problems to have a better understanding of their suffering and ways to discover a healthy, happy and peaceful lifestyle. I felt that when people had physical problems their doctors made suggestions about their diet and exercise so that they could help themselves but when they suffered from emotional problems they sent them to psychiatrists to get medications but did not guide them to improve their quality of life. In my opinion, medications were the last step and not the first step to deal with emotional problems. I wanted to help people by educating them about the dynamics of their emotional suffering so that they could learn skills to help themselves and their dear ones. I wanted them to learn that a crisis can be an opportunity to grow and feel optimistic, and that breakdowns could be transformed into breakthroughs. Finally with the help of my patients and my colleagues, Anne Henderson and Bette Davis, I was successful in creating a self-help program called Green Zone Living based on the Green Zone Philosophy.

In the last 10 years we have published five books and produced two videos to help our patients and their families. We have written them in easy to understand language and included the stories of our patients. The books in the Green Zone Series include:

1. *The Art of Living in your Green Zone*
2. *The Art of Loving in your Green Zone*
3. *The Art of Working in your Green Zone*
4. *Creating Green Zone Schools - The Art of Learning in your Green Zone, and*
5. *Green Zone Living - 7 Steps to a healthy, happy and peaceful lifestyle.*

The videos are:
1.   *Green Zone Stories, and*

2.   *Green Zone Lifestyles.*

These books and videos have helped numerous people by providing them hope and inspiration and teaching them life and social skills.

In this chapter I would like to discuss the basic ideas and concepts of the Green Zone Philosophy that is the foundation of this self-help program and Green Zone Therapy. Green Zone Philosophy was conceived and delivered in the Creative Psychotherapy Clinic which became its labor room.

I feel honored that my patients trusted me with their stories and gave me an opportunity to serve them. I learnt as much from them as they learnt from me. I would not have been able to create this Green Zone Philosophy if they were not my co-travelers in this professional journey.

GIVING BIRTH TO GREEN ZONE PHILOSOPHY

Being a creative person I am used to experiencing a wide range of creative moments, some minor, some major, some ordinary, some extraordinary, some simple, some profound. For me, they are all precious as they help me in developing insights into my personal, social and professional life. Those profoundly creative moments are associated with "aha" experiences. Those moments are special gifts as they change and transform my life and inspire me to grow. I remember experiencing one of those profoundly creative moments a few years ago during a psychotherapy session with a couple. I was most concerned about the episodes of domestic violence. Nancy, the wife shared with me that Bill, her husband of twenty years, verbally and physically abused her. She had given him an ultimatum, to get professional help or she would leave and file for divorce. Bill did not want to lose her so he agreed to see a doctor. Their family doctor referred the couple to me as he had referred many couples before to my clinic.

In the first couple of sessions I made an assessment of the dynamics of the relationship and tried to connect with the couple. It seemed as if the husband was genuinely interested in changing but did not know how. He had poor role models as a child and had grown up in an abusive family where his father was abusive to his mother.

Bill and Nancy had a 12 year old son. In the third session, Bill told me that he loved his son and called him 'Prince'. When I asked him, "Do you want to see your son become a prince?" he said, "Yes". I smiled and responded, "If you want your son to be a prince then you have to treat his mother like a queen. If you treat her like a slave, he will never be a prince." Bill smiled and that smile connected us. He realized that I was compassionate and was trying to help him.

In the next session I gently confronted him by asking, "How can you hurt the woman you love?' He seemed apologetic and said, "Dr. Sohail, I do not know what happens that I get triggered and lose control. I say and do things that I regret the next day. I apologize but after a few days I do the same thing all over again."

While I was listening to him, I stared in his eyes and said, "Bill, listen to me carefully. When you are driving and you see a yellow light, what do you do?"

"I put my foot on the accelerator."

"And why is that?"

"I am always in a hurry, in a hurry to go to work, and in a hurry to get home."

"Bill, when a wise man sees a yellow light, he puts his foot on the brake and not on the accelerator. A wise man stops and only goes forward when there is a green light. When you are angry you are in the Yellow Zone. You need to stop and wait and only go forward when you are in a relaxed and peaceful Green Zone, otherwise you will lose control and fall into the toxic Red Zone."

The next week when Nancy came she was thrilled.

"What did you do, Dr. Sohail? What did you say to Bill. You have performed a miracle. He is a changed man. He has not lost control in a whole week. I am so impressed."

I realized that Bill was ready to change and his love for Nancy and his trusting relationship with me helped him make that change possible.

I contemplated about that change and realized that the image of the Green, Yellow and Red traffic lights had a powerful potential. It was visual. It was effective. It helped people to develop self awareness as well as self control. I shared that concept with other couples and found it very helpful. That concept was the seed that grew in my mind and over the years, became a plant, then a tall tree which started bearing fruits. Those fruits are the series of concepts inter-linked in the Green Zone Philosophy. Such a philosophy has become the foundation of the

Self-Help program named Green Zone Living that Bette and I, use in our personal lives as well as in Green Zone Therapy that we practice in our professional life. Discovering and practicing Green Zone Philosophy has made our lives and the lives of many of our patients, colleagues and friends quite peaceful. It is our gift to the suffering humanity that helps people heal and grow and develop their fullest potential. Green Zone Philosophy helps us discover our inner peace and then join others to create peaceful relationships, families, workplaces and communities. I will share some of the basic concepts and principles of Green Zone Philosophy and Green Zone Therapy in the following pages.

3 EMOTIONAL ZONES - GREEN, YELLOW, RED
Green, Yellow and Red Zones are three imaginary Emotional Zones. The basic concept is that, like the traffic lights, all of us live in one of these three zones. When we are relaxed and happy and enjoying life, we are in our Green Zone, when we are mildly sad, frustrated and unhappy, we are in our Yellow Zone. When we get depressed, angry, lose control and become irrational, we are in our Red Zone. I am of the opinion that the awareness of our Emotional Zones is the first step towards improving our mental health and creating a healthy, happy and peaceful life that I call Green Zone Living.

The Green Zone concept is simple but multifaceted. When I say the Green Zone concept is simple, I mean it can be understood by children. Let me share a story with you. One day my poet friend, Rasheed Nadeem called to share with me that his 5 year old daughter, Afroze and 7 year old son, Imroze were fighting. Afroze was crying. When Nadeem went in the room to help them, Afroze said, "Dad, you go back to the living room. I cannot talk to you. I am in my Red Zone." After a few minutes she came to him and said, "Dad, I am in my Yellow Zone. I can talk how." When Nadeem asked her what pushed her to the Red Zone she told him that her brother broke her doll. When Nadeem asked her how he could help, she said, "Dad, if you promise to buy me a new doll, I will come to the Green Zone but if you do not promise, I will go back to my Red Zone." Nadeem laughed, gave her a big hug and promised to buy a new doll. Nadeem told me that his children use that model all the time, although to their advantage some times.

At the same time, the Green Zone Model is so multifaceted that our colleague, Rufi who is a manager, has incorporated it into his workplace. He has bought 60 Green, Yellow and Red flags for his 60 employees in their offices. They put the flag in an obvious place to let other people know what Zone they are in. During the day, when a staff member's mood changes, the flag changes. It helps colleagues to decide when they should approach others. When Rufi's boss was visiting from Los Angeles, he was quite impressed by those flags and suggested that he would like to introduce the Green Zone Model to their head office in America.

3 Rs - RECOGNIZING, RECOVERING, RESTRAINING
I share with my patients that one of the most significant principles of Green Zone Philosophy is that

the more we are aware of the changes in our Emotional Zones, the more we are able to control them and spend more time in our peaceful Green Zone. The concept of 3Rs puts that principle in action.

- The first R is Recognizing the changes in our Emotional Zones.
- The second R is Recovering from our Yellow and Red Zones.
- The third R is Restraining from going back to our Yellow and Red Zones.

The more people are aware of their emotional triggers the more they can deal with them and learn skills not to be affected by them. They learn that Green Zone people *ACT* while Red Zone people *REACT* in life.

I also bring to people's attention that their self esteem plays a key role in their mental health. People with poor self esteem are more vulnerable to suffer as they may be overly sensitive to other people's comments and criticisms.

Of all the psychologists and philosophers who discussed the issue of self-esteem, the one who impressed me the most was Harry Stack Sullivan, an American psychiatrist, who was one of the pioneers of the interpersonal school of psychiatry. He believed that poor self esteem was the corner stone of all emotional problems.

He developed the concept of *Good Me* and *Bad Me*. He believed that all those things that we like about ourselves are part of *Good Me* and all those things that we do not like about ourselves is part of *Bad Me*. For emotionally healthy people, Good Me is far bigger than Bad Me and in people with emotional problems, Bad Me is far bigger than Good Me. We need to help people with emotional problems make their Good Me bigger than their Bad Me. This can be done by helping them focus on their potentials, talents and their natural gifts to improve their self-esteem, self worth and self confidence.

People with poor self esteem are more vulnerable to be emotionally triggered by internal and external stimuli and react to stressors.

I have developed the concept of *other esteem* as compared to self esteem. Self esteem is the esteem that we develop ourselves and other esteem is the esteem that we rely on others to give us. People who rely on other esteem more than self esteem, are more vulnerable to be emotionally triggered and go to their Yellow and Red Zones because they are sensitive to the negative comments of their friends, colleagues and family members. On the other hand, those people whose esteem is not dependent on others and who can create their own esteem, feel more secure and are less affected by the negative comments of others.

3 WAYS TO DEAL WITH CONFLICTS-RESOLVE, DISSOLVE, MEDIATE

After spending more and more time in our peaceful Green Zone, we can focus on our relationships. I ask people that I work with to make a list of all their significant relationships and then decide which Zone each relationship is in. The relationships that live in the Yellow and Red Zones can be brought to the Green Zone if we discuss those issues with our dear ones. We can approach them suggesting that we can deal with our conflicts in three ways.

The first way is to *resolve* the conflicts by improving the quality of communication.

The second way is to *dissolve* the relationship and say goodbye to that person.

But if we do not want to dissolve the relationship we can suggest a mediator, whether a friend, a relative or a therapist that both parties respect to assist in resolving the relationship issues. Resolving, dissolving and mediating can save most relationships and increase the amount of time spent in the Green Zone.

One of the significant principles of Green Zone Philosophy is that Green Zone communication takes place when both parties are in the Green Zone. I share with my patients that there are Green Zone words that help communication and Red Zone words that hinder communication.

Let me share an example. One spouse leaves the office and gets stuck in traffic and reaches home late while the other spouse is waiting after cooking dinner. As he enters the house he says," I am sorry, I am late. I got stuck in traffic." Rather than being sympathetic she says, "You are *always* late" and he replies, "You are *never* sympathetic." *Always* and *never* are Red Zone words. Similarly, *Should* is a Red Zone word. It makes the other person feel like a child and an Adult to Adult communication changes to Parent-Child communication. The interaction can easily fall into the Red Zone as one person feels criticized by the other.

On the other hand, asking people what they would like to do, want to do and love to do keeps the relationship and communication in the Green Zone as these words are Green Zone words. Similarly affectionate words like *honey, sweetheart, my love,* are

Green Zone words as they keep the relationship and communication in a loving and peaceful space.

3 SYSTEMS - FAMILY, WORK, COMMUNITY
After dealing with relationships, we can focus on the social systems that we live in. There are three that are most important: Family, Work and Community. Like people and relationships, systems also live in Green, Yellow and Red Zones. Recognizing what Zone our systems live in not only prompts us to consider what we want to do to change them but how we can buffer ourselves when we enter them. Dealing with systems is particularly channeling, as systems are often emotionally stronger than individuals because we are out numbered. But evaluating our systems and making healthy changes are vital components of living in our Green Zone since it is hard to live in the Green Zone if your major systems are in the Red.

In our book, *The Art of Working in Your Green Zone,* Bette and I discuss how employees can transform a work environment from the Red Zone to the Green Zone or leave a toxic Red Zone to join a peaceful, healthy Green Zone workplace.

DISCOVERING OUR SPECIAL GIFT
Discovering our special gift is an integral part of Green Zone Philosophy. In my clinical practice, I meet so many people who have lost the connection with their dreams. They look and feel sad. When I review their lives, I find out that they have no goals, no ambitions, no ideals, no passions and no dreams. They do not live, they just exist. The more I get to know them and hear their stories, the more I discover

that they had dreams as teenagers, but as they grew older, they lost their dreams along the way.

After finishing school, they started looking for a job, got married, had children and got so involved in their day to day responsibilities that their lives became monotonous and boring. Their lives became too much work and too little play. And when they came to see me they realized they not only had lost their dreams but were also losing their hope. One woman said, "My future is a blank slate. I do not see anything."

I share with such people that all of us are born with a special gift and discovering that special gift is half of the struggle. Once we discover it then we need to nurture it so that it can grow to its fullest potential. Fortunate are those children who have parents and grandparents, aunts and uncles, teachers and principals, who pay special attention to them and recognize their talent and potential before they recognize it themselves.

My poet uncle, Arif told me that his aunt used to tell him, "The way you sit and hold your chin on your palm and stare in to space in deep thought, you will become a philosopher one day." My uncle was lucky to have such an aunt and I was lucky to have an uncle who nurtured my creativity and inspired me to become an artist, a humanist and a psychotherapist.

But what about all those people who did not have such nurturing and inspiring adults in their life? I believe we can discover our talent and special gifts even as adults, sometimes on our own, sometimes with the support of friends, and sometimes with the encouragement of therapists. Green Zone Therapy helps in that creative journey.

**3 PARTS THE OF SELF - NATURAL,
CONDITIONED AND CREATIVE**

The first part of the self is our *Natural Self* that we are all born with. Like the seed of a plant, all the potential is hidden in that seed. If that seed is nurtured then it grows to be a plant or a tree and bears fruit. Like a plant needs fresh air, rain and sunshine to grow, children need caring, love and discipline to become healthy adults who can not only work but also play. They find a balance in their lives and grow to their fullest potential.

Over time our Natural Self transforms into the second and third parts, the *Conditioned Self* and *Creative Self*. The Conditioned Self develops as a result of social, religious and cultural conditioning by our families and communities. This part of the Self is guided by *should, have to* and *must*. That is the part that helps us be responsible and carry on family and community traditions. On the other hand, the Creative Self develops when we follow our desires, wishes and ambitions. Such a part is guided by what we *like to, want to* and *love to do.*

Healthy, happy and peaceful people have found a balance between their Conditioned and Creative Self. Many people that we meet in our clinical practice have an overdeveloped Conditioned Self and an underdeveloped Creative Self. That is why they feel anxious, depressed and angry as their lives are guided by many *shoulds*. To develop their Creative Self, I suggest that they find an hour a day, a Green Zone Hour, in which they do what they love to do. That is the beginning of a hobby, and with the passage of time, that hobby becomes their passion and then transforms into a dream. Their lives become more enjoyable and meaningful. When I think of all the people who nurtured their Creative Self, I remember:

      - a man who became a photographer,

      - a woman who became a gardener,

      - another woman who became an expert in stained glass,

      - another man who became an accomplished musician, and

      - many who became inspiring writers.

3 ROADS TO A GREEN ZONE LIFESTYLE - CREATING, SHARING AND SERVING

I share with the people I work with, that after learning to have a Green Zone Day and Green Zone Week, if they want to further pursue the Green Zone Philosophy to create a Green Zone Lifestyle they need to follow three roads.

The first road is of *Creating* which they follow by developing their Creative Self. They create things that they enjoy.

The second road is of *Sharing*. After they have developed their creations, I ask them to share their creations with others and create a circle of friends, that I call the *Family of the Heart*. In that process, they make new friends and develop meaningful relationships with those people who have similar interests, passions and dreams. For me, it is the circle of my writer friends. We meet every week in a small group and every month in a big group. Each month we invite new members. Through the Internet we are connected with a very large group who stay in touch with us and read our creations.

Dr. K. Sohail/Bette Davis

The third road is *Serving*. After *Creating* and *Sharing* with close friends, I ask people to do some voluntary work to contribute their communities. I feel Green Zone people are well connected with their communities and serve them to become part of creating Green Zone Communities. Some like to lead and become Green Zone leaders, while others like to follow and become part of the team. Some have their own dream and some join others in their dream. Sometimes Green Zone people are able to create healthy and peaceful Green Zone islands in dysfunctional and toxic Red Zone seas, whether in the family, at work or in the community. When people start to recognize and appreciate their sincere efforts to create Green Zone Communities they join them and those islands become bigger and bigger. More and more people have the courage and strength to change their lives and transform the breakdowns of their families and communities into breakthroughs. They become part of creating a peaceful Green Zone World together.

At the end of therapy people recognize the essence of the Green Zone Philosophy. They realize that Green Zone Living is peaceful living. It starts with inner peace and ends in outer peace. People realize that emotional and social, political and cultural, national and international peace, are all connected in a mysterious way. Gradually, people learn to act locally and think globally. They develop a Green Zone relationship not only with their own families and communities, but also the whole humanity and discover unity in diversity.

To make it easier for people to understand the essence of Green Zone Philosophy and make it part of their lives, I share with them the following 12 Green Zone ideas.

GREEN ZONE IDEAS

1. Though human beings can be their own worst enemies, Green Zone Philosophy helps them become their own best friends.

As human beings, we all have a duality to our nature. We have a dark side and a bright side, a violent side and a peaceful side. At every turn in life and in every crisis, we make choices, some conscious, some unconscious. When we make unconscious and unhealthy choices, we become our worst enemies, but when we make conscious and healthy choices, we become our best friends. Green Zone Philosophy helps us stay in touch with our Green Zone so that we make wise and peaceful choices and become our best friends rather than our worst enemies.

2. Green Zone is the other name for a peaceful mind.

Those people who are in touch with their Green Zone feel connected with their peaceful centre, their inner voice, a reflection of their authentic self. Their mind becomes still like a lake that reflects the moon at night time. They act according to their convictions and do not feel guilty as they have a clear conscience.

3. Green Zone is our personal emotional thermometer.

Becoming aware of our Emotional Zones is the first step towards changing our lives for the better. The more we are aware of the changes, the more we are able to course correct ourselves.

Dr. K. Sohail/Bette Davis

Studies in biofeedback have helped us understand that when people are made aware of their bodily functions - breathing, body temperature and heart beat patterns - they developed more voluntary control over those functions which they previously believed were involuntary. The same theory applies to our emotional life. The more we are aware of the changes in our Emotional Zones, the more we are able to live in our peaceful Green Zone.

4.   *In the Yellow Zone, wise people put their foot on the brake rather than on the accelerator.*
The metaphor for the emotional Green, Yellow and Red Zones was inspired by the traffic lights because there are some similarities between emotional rules and traffic rules. Many people who get into angry and bitter fights with their dear ones and lose control do not stop themselves in their Yellow Zone. They do not recognize that they have a choice to go forward and have an accident or stop and avoid a crisis. The more people become aware of their Yellow Zone, the more they are able to make a U turn and come back to their peaceful Green Zone. In this way they do not risk landing in their painful Red Zone and losing control.

5.   *Green Zone Communication only takes place when both parties are in their Green Zone.*
When people who are in their peaceful Green Zone are interacting with people who are in their angry Red Zone, they do not realize that rather than bringing them out of their Red Zone, it is more likely that they would also fall into the Red Zone. People who are in their Red Zone act like drunks and throw angry bait that people who are in the Green Zone can easily bite.

It is wise for people who are in their Green Zone to wait until people who are in their Red Zone come back to their Green Zone so that both parties can engage in a fruitful discussion and a meaningful dialogue to share information and resolve conflicts peacefully and gracefully.

6.   *It is hard for people to stay in their Green Zone if they are part of a Yellow or Red Zone System, as systems are often emotionally stronger than individuals.*

It is not uncommon for peaceful Green Zone people to feel distressed if they are living with stressful families or working in toxic work environments. Sooner or later such environments pull people in to their negative vortex. If people have to live and work in such environments they need to create an Emotional Raincoat to decrease the negative effects. If possible it would be healthier to leave those environments and become part of peaceful Green Zone families and work systems.

7.   *Discovering one's special gift is a significant step towards creating a peaceful Green Zone Lifestyle.*

Life has given all of us a special gift. Some discover it sooner than others. The Green Zone Philosophy encourages people to have a Green Zone Hour everyday to do what they love to do. Such a process can start as a hobby and then progress into a passion and a dream. By sharing one's special gift one can also create a circle of friends, a Green Zone Family of the Heart. In these Green Zone relationships people bring out the best in each other.

8.   In Green Zone Families, every person's special gift is acknowledged and cherished.
Those people who grow up in neglectful Yellow Zone or abusive Red Zone families suffer for a long time. Fortunate are those people who grow up in nurturing and loving Green Zone families because in such families every person's special gift is acknowledged and cherished.

9.   Children need Green Zone families, schools and communities to become peaceful Green Zone adults.
It is our collective responsibility to make sure that all children that come into this world receive the love and care they need in their families, schools and communities to become peaceful Green Zone adults. It is part of folk wisdom that we need, 'a whole village to raise a child'. Children are our precious future. We need to take special care of them.

10. Serving humanity helps people to discover their Green Zone.
One does not need a Masters or a PhD in a caring profession to make a positive impact, all one needs is a caring mind and a compassionate heart.

11. Green Zone People are motivated by love and peace rather than hate, violence and war.
When we look around us, we find hate is becoming a powerful motivator. There are some leaders of social groups, religious organizations and political institutions who are fighting political and economic wars with violence and are rationalizing their hate by saying that they are promoting peace and social justice, democracy and human rights. They want to

promote peace by embracing violence. How sad! In the contemporary world we need more Green Zone people who are motivated by genuine love and peace.

12. When Green Zone People become leaders they inspire others to create Green Zone communities.
When Green Zone People become leaders of social groups, religious organizations or political institutions they inspire others. In the contemporary world we need more Green Zone leaders to take humanity to the next stage of human evolution.

Chapter Eight

Green Zone Philosophy Changed My Life - Interview with Barbara

Sohail: *Thank you very much for agreeing to be interviewed for this project on Green Zone Therapy. What do you remember about when you first came to see us? What were you struggling with?*

Barbara: I was very depressed. I'd been seeing Dr. Arfai for a couple of years I guess. But I'd been on anti-depressants for quite a long time. I just was not getting any better and I had a year of really rotten things happening to me that really knocked me down. I have been hospitalized twice before and I could recognize that I was just going down again. I was having a hard time. I think I was in a non-functioning state. I felt I wanted to crawl into a corner and not come out. I must have been very scared of crawling into the corner because I thought I would never come out. It was a very frightening feeling. Everything was out of control. My relationships were shot. I had lost my job. My daughter and her family had moved. My health was shot. It was just like there was nothing left. It's a good thing I was never suicidal. Dr. Arfai was only really offering medications, not offering psychotherapy. So he referred me to you. I was lucky I did not have to wait very long like other patients.

Sohail: *What were your expectations when you came here?*
Barbara: In the beginning I thought I would be patched up quickly and put back on my feet and just carry on with my life as I had before. I wasn't certainly looking for long term therapy. It wasn't on my radar at all. I didn't even know anybody did long term therapy other than things I read about long term psychoanalysis.

So when you and Bette offered to take me on as a patient I really thought that it was just going to be 6 months or so. In the beginning I thought we would be working on my depression but then gradually I realized I needed long term therapy for my personality problems.

Sohail: *What did you think when I offered you long term therapy?*
Barbara: One of the first things I can remember thinking was how long it was going to take me to make you understand my point of view; that my job was going to be to change you so that you could help me not change myself. I felt that how I was living was the only way there was, given the circumstances. I had to take care of Sean, I had to take care of my grandchildren, and therefore Sarah, I was stuck with my health problems and I couldn't change my birth family or history. So I guess the first thing that I learned was that it was **me** who got to change and that was a surprising thing and it still surprises me when it catches me off guard as I used to think that I had a fully integrated personality. You knew I was in

my 50s. I was not going to accept that I was doing it wrong all these years. It was a huge thing. It was hard for me to accept that changing was a good thing for me. I was worried that I would lose myself, that a calmer, gentle Barbara would not be me.

Sohail: *Alongside being depressed, you also struggled with anger. Can you tell me about your anger?*
Barbara: In the beginning I did not even think I was angry. Gradually I realized that I had been angry for a long time and everything made me angry. It was because of my self righteous attitude. I was angry at the world. I was angry about how my life had started and how it had continued.

Sohail: *You seemed to be a bit judgmental.*
Barbara: Yes, I was very judgmental. I also felt that this was my "last kick at the can." If I didn't get well now, I probably never would. One of the things I kept saying at the beginning was that it seemed everyone else had a list of life rules, or a map, so that they understood how to behave or act. I understand now that to compensate, I had made my own rules, but then expected everyone to follow them, which only increased my problems. Now I have created my own Green Zone "policy manual" and so long as I stay in my own Green Zone and don't get dragged into others' Red Zone, I'll be ok. Yes, I was very judgmental but didn't know I was. I believed people did not do what they were supposed to do. As I got better I started to feel other feelings, other than anger. I felt shame and regret. When I came for therapy I was a very extreme person.

Sohail: *How did you feel when you were introduced to the Green Zone Philosophy?*

Barbara: I thought it was great because it was very visual. I could see clearly that Green is good, Yellow is not so great and Red is, 'Watch out, Barbara is in town!' But it didn't hit me emotionally because I was not in touch with my emotions. But when I got in touch with my emotions it felt better. I started having Green Zone emotions. What's that saying, 'nothing succeeds like success'. Once you start to feel good then you want to do it more and then it becomes a lot clearer. Finally, it becomes a self diagnostic test and you ask yourself when you are turning on the engine whether it is in the Green and if not why not.

Sohail: *So do you remember when you got to the stage when you were no longer angry?*

Barbara: What last week? (Laughing) I can remember when I first realized that I had a feeling other than anger. But initially I could only say I was 'not angry'. I didn't know what the feeling was specifically but I was not angry. The major shift in my anger happened nearly 18 months ago when I started waking up and my fist was not clinched and my stomach was not in a knot. And then it happened more and more that I woke up feeling calm.

Sohail: *If a friend you had not seen for a few years saw you now as a calm and peaceful person and asked you how did therapy help you, what would you tell her?*

Barbara: Listening. Listening, more than anything. Having someone saying to me over and over and over again that I am an okay person and I can become a better person, a happier person helped me. Therapy provided me with positive messages and a map that I did not have before. So the first half was listening and the second half was checking myself, before I did anything. Learning to check was a big deal. Instead of going out and doing it, then coming back and saying, "Oh, I shouldn't have done that". It helped having a teacher, whether you fit as a parental teacher or a professorial teacher, having somebody to show me the way, having a guide. I know I couldn't do this on my own. I always say to other patients in group therapy that showing up is what you have to do to get more than a patch up job.

Sohail: *How do you see your life different today than 5 years ago? What is the fundamental difference for you?*
Barbara: I love my husband. I mean that's the biggest difference. I really do. I still don't like him some days (laughing). He's still a pain and all the things I said about him are still true, but they are only a part of it now. They are not all of him, so that's the biggy. My relationships with all of my family, and all my siblings have improved. I still miss the closeness that I had with mom before I got myself in such a state. I really miss that, but I'm learning to build a different relationship with her that isn't false. I'm learning to have Green Zone relationships within a Red Zone system.

Sohail: *How is your self image changed over the years?*
Barbara: That's the last part that is still a bit wobbly. I like myself more now. I didn't know that I didn't like myself before. I'm not as confident as I used to be and I miss that. I miss being a real self confident person but that self confidence was false. It used to get me

into a lot of trouble and some of it was actually booze. I understand now that what I thought was self confidence was really the opposite, like most things, it was only surface.

Sohail: *Did your self confidence have a touch of arrogance?*
Barbara: It did. I used to believe I was the best person in the room and now I'm willing to admit that there might be other people who are as good as me. Humour! But I don't need to be the best. I just have to be me.

Sohail: *So you have developed some humility?*
Barbara: Yes, some humility. Humility is a good thing. I used to be arrogant. But looking back on arrogance I think it was good in a way because it got me through some tough things as I needed it some time. I needed arrogance to feel that I was the best person to do that job.

Sohail: *Do you feel any change in your sense of compassion in the last year?*
Barbara: Yes, and that's hard. That's probably the hardest feeling to develop. To be compassionate and see somebody hurt and feel that pain and not be able to do anything about it. It's hard. But being able to emotionally comprehend how my actions and manner impacted others has been really good.

Sohail: *What about developing some recreational and creative interests?*
Barbara: That's still a struggle but it's becoming a quest rather than a chore. I'm looking for something

that will give me fulfillment. Make me feel good. Something that I can enjoy, not something that is work. This is a new thought for me. I really haven't had a lot of time to play and I don't know how to play. It is not something I know what to do with.

Sohail: *But you're learning?*
Barbara: Yes, I'm learning. It's a lot of dipping into something and trying it and having an enthusiasm and then realizing, 'No, maybe that's not what I want to do!' But I do know that I don't want to work. I feel a bit guilty about it because I feel I should want to go to work or I should want to do volunteer work, I should want to give something or do something but I don't. I have worked since I was 12 and I haven't done a lot of volunteer work but I have done a lot of work that other people do as volunteers. I had been taking care of my mom on top of going to work and raising a family, which included caring for a son who was born with a significant and continuous need for medical care. I am also learning about duty and what I feel I 'should' do. I am realizing that I do things for other people that are for their benefit, not mine, and it only becomes a "Duty" if I approach it as a Red Zone thing. If I approach it in my Green Zone, I can get pleasure from giving them pleasure. I understand that it's ok to do the fun thing first. I have also realized that the lethargy I was associating with depression was tied to that feeling of still having to do the "shoulds" (Duty) and if I wasn't doing my duty then I couldn't do anything else. So right now I don't feel a need to do anything that comes under that category.

Sohail: *On a scale of one to ten, ten being the best and one the worst, where do you think you were when you came here and where are you now?*

Barbara: I was as low as you can be when I came here, maybe 1 in my opinion. Now that I live in my Green Zone I am a 9. Sometimes even 10 when I'm humming along. There are days I am an 8 or 7 but I rarely go to the Red Zone and if I go, I quickly recover.

Sohail: *How do you feel having two therapists - me and Bette, in group and individual therapy rather than one therapist? How was that experience for you?*

Barbara: Well, I thought it was great. I can't imagine what it would be like to only have one therapist. There was never ever a time I sat here and wished it was only one of you, but you know it might be easier if it was just one or it might be less intense. It was never a time when I wished that there was only one person. So to me it was ideal and I think it made me feel cared for. I don't know whether I would have felt cared for even when there was one therapist. I sometimes wonder whether I could manipulate one therapist. I know I can't manipulate you both. (Both laughing). Perhaps because of the abandonment I had because of my early childhood, it helped having two "parents."

Sohail: *So you thought you got the right match with your therapists?*

Barbara: Yes

Sohail: *What advice would you give other people now who are having personality problems and contemplating going into therapy?*

Dr. K. Sohail/Bette Davis

Barbara: I would tell them to come and sit in your waiting room and refuse to leave until they got an appointment. I would recommend that to anybody who is having trouble with their life that they should get therapy.

Sohail: *Do you feel different about Green Zone Philosophy now than when you were first introduced to it?*
Barbara: When I was first got introduced to it, it was just a concept. It seemed so simple. It was like taking an emotional temperature. It was like saying, "Today I am in the Green Zone. Yesterday I was in the Yellow Zone because this happened and this happened and this happened but now I'm in the Green Zone because I did this and this and this," but it took a lot of work and time to fully integrate it, and it may never be fully natural. If people learn it early they could have healthier lives.

Sohail: *That's why we are now introducing it into the schools to teenagers so that they can learn about mental health and Green Zone Philosophy at an early age.*
Barbara: That would be so good. It will also help to reduce the stigma about mental illness in our schools and communities. I used to hide that I received therapy but now I can tell people and not feel embarrassed. I like the language of the Green Zone.

Sohail: *Yes, Green Zone Philosophy can help move away from that stigma because of its language.*
Barbara: So you need not say you are depressed, instead you can say, you're in your Red Zone?

Sohail: *It gives people a choice. They can use traditional terminology or use Green Zone terminology that is not judgmental.*
You were also planning to move to a new town. How do you feel about that?
Barbara: I think I can take care of myself without support. But that's being a little bit arrogant again, isn't it. (Laughing) It's like saying my back doesn't hurt today so I can train and run a marathon. It doesn't matter what I do I will never be able to train and run a marathon. So part of me has to accept the fact that I'm always going to be a little bit fragile but, yes I do I feel I don't need to come in every week to make sure that I'm staying in the Green Zone. I feel confident that I can recognize when I'm going into the Red and that mostly I know what to do about it. I did not have impulse control before but now I have it.

Sohail: *So you became wiser over the years.*
Barbara: Wiser I have become, Yoda.

Sohail: *Thank you very much for sharing your story.*
Barbara: Thank you for all the help you provided me and thank you for introducing me to Green Zone Philosophy that changed my life.

LETTER TO BARBARA

Dear Barbara,
Thank you for sharing your Green Zone Story. When I was reading your interview I was remembering the time when Bette and I saw you for the first time, referred by Dr Arfai, for group therapy. During the assessment I realized that, although you were referred

for depression, you also suffered from serious personality problems that needed long term psychotherapy. I was quite aware that most psychiatrists offer medications and most therapists offer short term psychotherapy for crisis intervention. I feel proud that our Green Zone Clinic offers long term individual, couple, family and group therapy for personality and family problems. But I did not mention that to you in the beginning as I did not want to scare you. But as you felt comfortable with the other group members and us as therapists, I suggested long term therapy. In the beginning you were surprised but then you saw the wisdom in it.

It did not take me long to realize that you had a 'should personality', as you had strong views about many things and you were quite self righteous. Although you were a humanist, you had a judgmental attitude like some religious people who are obsessed with right and wrong, good and bad, black and white. Your judgmental attitude got you in many interpersonal conflicts and pushed people away.

With the passage of time in therapy, you realized that your depression was intimately connected with your anger. The more you got in touch with your anger, the more you could share it and express it in therapy and let go. I remember the time you got so angry with me that you angrily stomped out of my office because I had disagreed with your ideas. There were also times you criticized me as you felt that I was not running group therapy the way it 'should' be run.

As we worked through our conflicts in therapy and you let your anger go, the deeper aspects of your personality came to the surface. Your personality was like an orange - bitter peel, sweet pulp. Your angry Red Zone was covering the sweet Green Zone of your personality.

Many therapists, like Sigmund Freud, do not accept patients for long term therapy after 40, as they feel that the personality has become so fixed and rigid that it cannot be changed. But I do not agree with that philosophy. I believe that at any age if the person is motivated to change, that person should be given a chance. So when you came to see us you were 50. That was one reason why it was hard for you to change. But you worked very hard and you did change for the better.

I want to congratulate you for becoming a kinder and gentler Green Zone Person. Now you are less judgmental and more accepting of people. You have become a forgiving person who overlooks people's faults, mistakes and shortcomings. I am so proud of you as you have become a loving daughter, wife, mother, grandmother and a friend. Now you are compassionate to other group members. I am impressed by the changes you have made. I am sure your story will become a source of inspiration for many readers. Thanks for sharing your Green Zone Story.

Sincerely, Sohail
July 21st, 2010

Dr. K. Sohail/Bette Davis

Chapter Nine

Tonia's Green Zone Story

Everyone has a story of heartache and hardship. Someone hurt them along the way and they let it bog them down, each day reliving the pain, allowing it to linger and affect their ability to move forward and see what the world has to offer. Because what the world offers us, can only be obtained with our own reach. I made the choice to grab it eight years ago when I was ready to let go of the pain, depression and anxiety; I will never return again.

I could go to great lengths describing the hurt I felt from family members who put me down both verbally and spiritually. I could tell you the many stories of the heartache I went through for six and a half years in a controlling and verbally abusive relationship that left me stripped of my identity and many lost years of my youth. I could tell you of the recurring depression and anxiety that I experienced even after releasing myself from the shackles of that controlling relationship. Or the relay race of medications I tried and went off only to realize that I didn't need any of them. There were and still are battles with my family for my non-traditional lifestyle and life choices. But to me what has brought me out of the deepest holes of darkness and is more important than reliving a past that is gone and cannot be changed, is the ability to put one's life into perspective. Even more important is the ability to express oneself in a creative way.

Growing up in a traditional household, as a creative and extroverted person, had its challenges. At a young age I made friends very easily while my sister sat close by with a book in hand. As I grew up I was immersed in environments that restricted my social side. I began to isolate myself from my family in order to avoid taking on their behaviours that I did not want. This continued for years. The cycles of isolation led me to fall in and out of depression and anxiety beginning as young as ten years old and progressed as the years passed. Having little encouragement from my parents I never participated in any extra curricular activities in high school, which I desperately needed. Every time I tried to express interest in things I wanted to do, my family shot the idea down and told me I was crazy. Not being able to be myself took a toll on me. For many years, and still to this day, my family does not accept the real me. This led me to a loss of self which inevitably lead me to my depression and anxiety.

As I grew into my twenties and the depression continued. My relationship with my parents worsened as they pushed me away and continued to try and control my life. It got to the point of me wanting to end my life on a daily basis and that was when I finally decided to get help. It was the best decision I ever made in my life. I went to my doctor at 24 years of age and told her I thought I was suffering from depression. After some assessment she agreed with my diagnoses and from there I was referred to the Creative Psychotherapy Clinic.

Unfortunately there was a one year waiting list to see Dr. Sohail but I was certain this was the right place and continued to call and check in every now and then. After about four months of waiting and things getting worse, it was suggested I see Bette Davis who is a seasoned mental health nurse and Dr. Sohail's co-therapist.

This is when my road to therapy began, one that saved my life. To put it quite simply, Bette Davis saved my life, more than once. She saw where I was and what I needed, she took the extra time and care that helped bring me out of the deepest depressions, overwhelming panic attacks and severe anxiety. I remember the first few years calling her on her cell phone as well as emailing her when I had no one else to lean on. She was the supportive mother and teacher I longed for who would teach me what I already internally knew. She taught me the basics about how to live a healthy life which included healthy boundaries with people, finding my natural rhythm, effectively communicating with others, decision making, how to manage my life and most importantly she helped me deal and process all of the hurt and pain that had accumulated over the years. The many lessons she taught me were always explained with such visual metaphors that they allowed me to reflect outside of our sessions and helped me remember what I needed to focus on. She has seen me grow over the last eight years and I can walk away now from our relationship satisfied and grateful for everything that occurred.

My therapy process was quite diverse in that I did not just see Bette for the length of my therapy. When I was at my worst and refused to go into the hospital, Bette suggested that I attend weekly group therapy sessions lead by her and Dr. Sohail. I agreed, having no problem talking to others, especially when it came to my problems. Although I am an extrovert the nature of my depression and anxiety lead me to have few people I could count on. The ones I could talk to could only listen to so much of my despair. Going to group was another saving grace for me in that it provided me with the support, understanding, guidance and belonging I needed. For the four years I attended, I missed only a handful of sessions, and although I was not *in focus* each week I would leave each time with a handful of wisdom and the feeling that I was not alone. It also allowed me to gage where I was at in my growth and path and I was able to share my own wisdom with others. I felt respected and liked which inevitably everyone wants and needs. When I was ready to leave the group, I was sad to leave those who had helped me through so much, but I have created my own 'family of the heart' that I could depend on for support and companionship.

The last piece of my therapy was with Dr. Sohail and it was a very different path. I met him at the beginning of my therapy once I had already begun to see Bette. We met a few times but I did not connect and I soon decided that I would continue with Bette. As my time with Bette came to an end it was suggested that I work with Dr. Sohail in order to take advantage of being able to work with a male therapist. This would allow me to work out the rest of my issues. Having worked with Dr. Sohail in group therapy, the process with him was quicker also because I already had done a great deal of work before hand. He pushed me to step out of my comfort zone and his dynamic but supportive feedback made me really think and challenge my old belief systems. I had dealt with so much toxic waste with Bette I was now better able to reflect and focus on the few remaining issues with Dr. Sohail. I learned to own who I was and not be afraid to speak my mind.

My overall experience at the clinic was one that I am thankful for. It was their kind and genuine approach that kept me going but also their desire to make things simple for people. The Green Zone approach is one that allows individuals to easily identify challenging situations and to learn tools to approach them in a healthy way. I learned quickly that Red Zone environments played a huge role in my depression and anxiety as well as the Red and Yellow Zone relationships I had been in. I love their approach so much I have used it in the classroom when teaching health to students. I also used the Green Zone approach in a series of seven paintings to depict my growth from a Red Zone shell and environment to moving towards a Green Zone life and letting go of the Red and Yellow past. I first used the theory in a painting titled, "Almost There" to depict my path from Red to Green and the gradual progression to living a more emotionally stable life. Dr. Sohail and Bette liked it so much that they purchased it to hang in their clinic. Expressing myself through art has definitely been key and I continue to push myself and am working towards being a professional artist.

It was not an easy road and it seems quite simple to just express who you are. But first you must know who you are and what you are made of. Allowing others to define you can be detrimental to your being. Exploring the world and taking what it has to offer is a better way to come to that realization. I spent many years fearful and anxiety-ridden which left me socially crippled. I was not open-minded or strong enough to go out and do different things. However, the more you do, the better you feel, and this has also been key to my moving forward. I found staying home alone only made matters worse because I lived inside my head instead of the world around me.

Another big challenge was the self pity I lived day in and day out. Very often we repeat behavours and thought patterns so much that we don't even realize how detrimental they are to our being. Feeling sorry for myself only held me back from moving forward and pushed others away. It is easy to blame others and to feel like the victim. It is easy to feel like you have no control over your life so that you do not have to take responsibility for the actions you took to get where you are. I now live by the motto, 'If you don't like it, do something about it'. I have no one to blame but myself if something doesn't work out but I am kind enough to myself that I know things do not always work out as planned and mistakes lead to knowledge and growth.

Having moved to Toronto three months ago has allowed me to foster my creative self in every way. I now own who I am and that means finding a place to live that reflects who I am. I feel that who I am is nurtured here with what surrounds me. My time here has only begun and the endless options and opportunities keep me energized and alive. However, life is an ever evolving process and I am still working with my family to establish healthy, connected relationships. While some times are better than others,

I still have to reiterate my life choices and remind my parents that I am an adult who has control over my life. I am also still on a journey to become friends and equals with my sister, who was emotionally abusive to me growing up and still has the habit of taking her frustrations out on me and others. But because of Bette and Dr. Sohail I now have the tools I need for a healthy life, and I know how to use them.

There are many truths to life yet I feel that there are basic concepts that help one live a happy and healthy life both mentally and spiritually. Being sure of what you want in life allows you to take charge instead of putting fault on others and asking for their guidance before you know what you want. Prioritizing and focusing on a few goals at a time is far more productive than trying to be a super hero. Taking your time in life also helps solidify relationships, goals, change and growth. I am a leader who is socially drawn to people and I thrive on telling my story to inspire others to find themselves which leads to true happiness. The lessons continue to come and I continue to move forward. I could express more of what brought me here today but that is my road and what worked for me. My best words of advice are to continue to make goals and work on them until you have reached them or decide that they are not what you want. Most of all, know who you are and find ways to express it each day.

LETTER TO TONIA

Dear Tonia,

In my mind I have a very clear picture of you in the first months of our work together in therapy. You were emotionally incapacitated as you moved from severe anxiety and panic attacks to crippling depression. My hope and the challenge in those days was to relieve those symptoms to the extent that we might work on the deeper issues of self-esteem and your dysfunctional and often abusive relationships. Thankfully, we created a very effective therapeutic relationship as I felt quickly connected to you and you to me. That connection was a miraculous feat for a person who had endured so much abuse and dysfunction in her primary relationships. I so admired the courage you showed, to not only connect but be vulnerable, in therapy.

You took the therapeutic process seriously. True to the values of your teaching profession you always did your homework. Despite your attention and concentration struggles, so severe that you often had to take notes in our sessions to read later when you were more able to focus, you rarely missed an appointment in individual or group therapy. Although you struggled in the earlier years with being too detail oriented, you still did not avoid the opportunity to be *in focus* in group therapy. Whether you were in focus so that you were sharing an issue to get the groups feedback, or you were contributing your support and feedback, you became a valued group member. Over time, members new to the group, were drawn to you as a role model.

Dr. K. Sohail/Bette Davis

Each person with whom I have worked in therapy stands out in unique ways. For you, I was always fascinated by the number of times you would do things that were not in your best interests, that we had discussed many times and agreed they were not in your best interest and yet you would do them. For example, going to Italy by yourself in the height of your anxiety and depression to stay with your unknown but dysfunctional family, or just getting stabilized on a medication to reduce your anxiety or depression and then coming off it. Most clients in these situations feel distressed by agreeing to one thing and doing another, so much so that they often disconnect from therapy and the therapist. Amazingly, you never did. You would come to a session or phone from Italy to discuss what you had done and the lessons you were learning. You never gave up on you or on our relationship. As you say, you were always trying to find out who you are and to discover ways to express your wonderful uniqueness.

I feel so privileged to have been a part of your journey as you accomplished your goals, and in your own creative style. Professionally, our relationship and the expansiveness of the work we achieved, has been very gratifying as well as a valuable opportunity to grow as a therapist. I am so proud of the complex and challenging work you have done. You very much deserve to be proud of yourself!

With admiration and warmth,

Bette

Chapter Ten

Richard's Green Zone Story

My Green Zone story is my own, but I have come to understand it through the help of many others, including Bette Davis, Khalid Sohail, my wife Julie, a couple of very close friends, and the very understanding and supportive set of Grouptherapy participants, whom I labeled as my 'Secret Friends' in a song I wrote in 2009. More about that later in this article.

I originally discovered the Green Zone Creative Psychotherapy Clinic in 2005, when my wife Julie and I arrived here after trying several other support options through my employer's Employee Assistance Program (EAP), over the course of 1-2 years.

Julie and I had been experiencing relationship issues. We were disconnected, drifting along, without a sense of a unified purpose, and I was feeling isolated and alone. I had a hard time expressing myself to her since we were in a disconnected state, and because she was my primary confidante, I felt completely isolated and alone. I have long had difficulty with conflict, and it was too easy for me to avoid the potential conflict of addressing this situation openly. In discussions with each other, it seemed that we too easily would 'dig in' to our respective positions rather than seeing the other person's perspective. Julie was becoming more and more independent, of which I had always been encouraging. However, more and more, it felt like this independence was not including me.

Once we arrived at the Green Zone clinic, I found the experience to be a positive and enlightening one. I have always wanted to be able to openly share what is 'going on inside me', however I have always been very selective with whom I confided personal details and feelings. Julie had always been one of those people, but with our situation, I did not feel that I even had that anymore. In our sessions with Bette and Sohail, I felt a sense of comfort and trust. These were two people who definitely cared about us as patients and as parents. We had two children in the mix as well. Yet, Bette and Sohail were also ones to not hold back, to be open and honest with us about our situation. It was all very well for us to explain our feelings and concerns, but what actions were we to take to do something with our situation? As I recall, it seemed we were only a few sessions in to our process, when the suggestion was made that we should consider temporarily spending some time apart. By separating ourselves from each other for an unspecified period of time we would have the ability to more clearly think about the circumstances and our own feelings. This would then help us respectively determine whether we wanted to still be together with the other person, or not. By knowing this, it would then provide a basis of what the next steps would become, either working to stay together or working on being apart. It was important to let the outcome of this temporary separation process determine what the next step would be and not to let it be a preconception that we would simply remain apart, which is most often what people assume.

For Julie and I, the step of a temporary separation was a scary situation to contemplate. But in reality I think we both knew that it made the most sense as well. For me, I knew deep down that it was the change that would really shake up our 'sitting on the fence'. Which was what we had been doing, whether we realized it or not. At that time, Julie and I had been in our uncertain world for about two years, and we had actually discussed a couple of times the idea of living apart and even took some initial actions on two occasions. Thus, I think we knew that it was the action needed this time. However, it was still very, very difficult to take this step, especially telling our children. The impact this might have on them was our greatest concern.

We both knew that the telling of the story to our children would be the hardest part. We had always ensured that we were civil to each other, which I think really helped us show our children that we were not doing something traumatic. We were doing something with the intention of making things better, even though it might seem a bit scary with only one of Mom or Dad at home during this period. The kids responded well, though we could tell they were a bit wary. We told them on a Sunday, that I would leave starting about a week later. This was to ensure they had some time to process it, but not too much time as to become very worried about it or for anyone to try to change our mind.

Julie and I had originally intended to be apart a week at a time. She would stay at her sister's nearby, and I would stay at my brother's home. We did not tell many people, perhaps one person each outside of those we would live with. After the first few days, we changed the arrangement to stay away for only half a week at a time. This worked out better with respect to the impact on the kids, since neither of us would be away for a long period. We were fortunate in that we had two siblings who could support us so well and that we could adjust the separation duration to best fit with our kids' situation. We were really able to insulate them from our situation causing a significant change to their lives.

During our separation, we both continued to see Bette and Sohail in a weekly session, though separately this time. We were asked to continue to write our thoughts as the process evolved and to bring them to discuss at our sessions. I learned from Sohail about 1 or 2 weeks into the separation process, that after about 2 days, Julie had written to Sohail and Bette that she really now understood that she wanted to stay with me. While I was happy to hear this at the time, I was also very skeptical that this was Julie's real answer. Was this just not remorse and regret talking? We had been going through our issues for 2 years by that time, and I could not believe that she could suddenly know her true feelings in 2 short days. Sohail seemed to believe her feelings were sincere. For me, I still needed more time to know what my real feelings were. I took several more weeks to get to a place where I really knew that I wanted to be together with Julie. I had always thought this was what I wanted, but with the ups and downs of 2 years, I really needed to be sure. In the end, we were separated for 4 weeks.

Once we were back under the same roof, we needed a lot of ongoing support and strategies to ensure we did not fall back into some of the old traps. We set aside specific time in a week to ensure we talked openly and honestly on various topics. There were topics we were eager and happy to share, but also ones that were a concern to us or had made us feel 'Yellow' or 'Red'. And we continued to meet with Bette & Sohail in separate sessions. Slowly but surely, we made progress and got to a point, after about a year, that Julie chose to discontinue attending sessions. I continued to attend on my own, though now on a monthly basis. It has now been about 3 years since that point, and I can say that Julie and I continue to be in a very good spot from a relationship perspective. We are very open with each other, appreciate the others' perspective, and don't take things personally as we did in the past. Situations of disagreement are just that, situations of disagreement. They are no longer situations that make me question our relationship and wonder whether we should stay together 'this time'. As such, therapy has been very positive for overcoming our relationship issues. It has also been positive for other reasons too.

In one of my personal sessions with Bette and Sohail, I was asked about whether I might be interested in attending a Group therapy session. I was initially a bit skeptical as it brought up visions of *The Bob Newhart Show*, and maybe it meant I had some kind of 'real problem'. However, I was also intrigued about what I might learn there, both about therapy and about myself. I also felt, deep down, that there was something more to me that I could learn and would learn, if I went to Group. Being of open mind, I signed on to try it out.

Group therapy has been a very life changing experience for me. I was initially slow to open up to the group and careful of what I would say, as I felt my way along in this new element. However, I could feel the trust that was being placed in each of us to hear people's stories and to provide feedback to them, without judgments. One of the things I was now exploring about myself were my feelings of inadequacy, low self esteem, and lack of confidence. Several times I have been able to share my feelings and have found solace, comfort, and have learned from the feedback people have given to me. So many times, the thoughts I pick up from the person who is 'in focus' and the thoughts I get from the feedback being given, get translated into something that is just so highly applicable in my own life. I have often thought that, 'the reason you initially came to Group is not the reason you are here'.

At the same time, I had started to explore my creative side with a deeper interest and passion than I had done in the past. In fact, I came to realize that my creativity was always something that had been present but I had pushed it down to another spot while I gave more attention to other areas of my life such as my work and my family. And Group has provided me an avenue to explore and to share my creativity.

I have had a strong interest in music all of my life and have had a guitar that I have dabbled with since I was 25 years old. In recent years, I had taken a renewed interest in playing it and even took guitar lessons again for a year. In the spring of 2007, the tragic passing of my nephew, Michael, led me to a point where I created my first original song. It was very hard emotionally that week to extricate the feelings that were inside of me out into another form, which was my first song. But when it happened, I somehow changed. I wrote several songs later that same year and have written 8 in total now. With some encouragement I have shared many of my musical creations with my group-mates. One song, 'Secret Friends' is a song about what I get from being in group. I have posted it to You-Tube and played it for friends. The feedback has been so positive. And I have felt so good about doing this. I realize that I would not likely have pushed myself so far creatively, had it not been for therapy and group. Not to mention, I have an audience who is very receptive to my work.

With the confidence I gained in these musical endeavors, I signed up for a *League of Rock* session in May 2010. *League of Rock* is a 10 week program, where one is merged into a band with other musicians of various instrumental capabilities. You choose 3 songs, and over the weeks rehearse them, perform 2 onstage workshops, receive feedback from industry professionals, record a song in a studio, and have a final Showcase performance in a club in Toronto. I engulfed myself in the experience, and can say that it was one of the greatest things I have ever done in my life. I think others can attest that I changed quite a lot with this experience. I focused on something that was for 'me'. And I had the support of my family and my workplace (i.e. my boss) to make sure I did not waver in my focus on this venture. I returned to group later this summer to share my experience, and shared my Band's recording and one of the other of the 3 songs. I can say I would never have taken the leap if it had not been for the strength and confidence I received from group. Today still, I find my time at group puts my mind in an open spot such that I am constantly sensing ideas for future songs.

As I look back on my time in therapy these past several years, for me it has been a very positive experience. I have learned much about myself and how I am. I know there is and likely will be always more to learn and know. However, therapy has provided me with some very valuable tools and skills for my Green Zone journey.

Secret Friends

I really need my secret friends
I really need my secret friends
To help me breathe and help me feel
They help me look inside myself
And figure out my life
I'm going to see my secret friends
I'm going to see my secret friends
To share some tales; to open up myself
Or maybe see a piece of me
In someone else's life.

Chorus:
Emotional oxygen
Emotional oxygen
Breathing in and breathing out
Emotional oxygen

When I see my secret friends
When I see my secret friends
I don't worry 'bout what they say
I hope they see a piece of me
In their own life
I'm thankful for my secret friends
I'm thankful for my secret friends
They give me comfort and a place
To say the things I'm afraid to say
In my daily life.

Chorus:
Emotional oxygen
Emotional oxygen
Breathing in and breathing out
Emotional oxygen

I know I'll leave my secret friends
I know I'll leave my secret friends
When I find that I can say
The things I know I have to say
In my own life.

Dr. K. Sohail/Bette Davis

Chapter Eleven

From the Depths of My Red Zone to the Peaks of My Green Zone - Neil's Green Zone Journey

I have discovered and embraced my Green Zone. My Green Zone is inclusive of my life at home with my wife, Kelly and young son, Nick, my work life, and my "Family of the Heart". The percentage of time that I spend in my Green Zone has increased significantly in the past five years. I have been visiting Dr. Sohail for five years of regular weekly sessions. These visits coupled with my hard work and determination have allowed me to travel from the depths of my Red Zone to the peaks of my Green Zone. This journey has been extremely difficult and challenging but rewarding.

I have created a Green Zone space around me with defined boundaries. Doing this has allowed me to take more charge of my life. I can now make important choices and decisions in a rational and healthier manner. I used to second guess a lot of my choices and underestimate myself in my decision making abilities. I rarely do that now. I am learning to act in my Green Zone rather than react in my Red Zone. I have learned a lot about myself, others in my life, and more about how important it is to have and maintain a mentally positive and healthy approach to everyday life. It is not easy to do this all the time though. At times, I have to consciously remove myself from my Red Zone and travel to my Green Zone. I have learned through Green Zone teachings not to park in my Red Zone but to drive out of it as quickly as possible. Recovering from time spent in my Red and Yellow Zones coupled with discovering my Green Zone has created a more positive outlook in my world.

Nowadays, I wake up in the mornings ready to start the day in my Green Zone. If I am not in the Green Zone at the start of my day I devise a plan in my mind to get there based on my years of hard work in therapy. I live everyday within my means and within the boundaries of my Green Zone. However, I am always looking to expand these boundaries.

I first met Dr. Sohail, Bette Davis, and Anne Henderson at their clinic in July 2005. I went through three years of individual counseling prior to meeting Dr. Sohail and his colleagues. My counselor, Sheila was very helpful and effective but I needed even more support than she could offer. I was introduced to the Green, Yellow, and Red Zone concept within weeks of starting my journey with Dr. Sohail. I attended weekly group meeting at his clinic until 2007. The group sessions were very helpful and enlightening but the time commitment caught up with me and I stopped attending. However, group therapy made me realize that many others out there had issues and struggles in their lives which were parallel or quite similar to mine.

I easily identified with the Red Zone. I lived most of my life in the Red Zone up to that point. I was born, raised, and publicly schooled in a small town in

Southern Ontario. In retrospect, my experiences as a child and teenager in my hometown were part of my Red Zone. I was a colored person from an immigrant family growing up in a predominantly 'white' town. I encountered racism in the form of verbal abuse and physical abuse throughout my fourteen years of school there. At home, I had dictating parents and emotionally distant siblings: my sister, Ann and my brother, Rob. I am the youngest offspring of my parents and I was expected to demonstrate at least the same academic performance as my siblings. I generally had a Red but sometimes Yellow Zone relationship with my four immediate family members. My siblings were quite self serving. Their selfish and competitive nature coupled with my father's iron fisted 'control' of his family limited my creative potential. My childhood shaped me to be rather insecure, lacking confidence, and superficially living life happily. Love, respect, and affection were very superficial during my childhood. I became a programmed academic student and an obedient son. I was a 'parent pleaser' and generally a 'people pleaser'. I did not discover my true identity, I was just Paul and Sue's son. I did not like myself nor my life.

I was looking for some kind of positive change. My years away at university were not what I envisioned. I lived for three years with my brother in a townhouse that my parents purchased. Rob and I were attending different universities in the same town. Being an obedient son to my parents I accepted this living arrangement as there was financial benefit for me. I give full credit to my parents for providing me with financial support. As I have grown, I believe that emotional support is far more important than financial support. I would have rather been 'broke' and emotionally healthy. The first few months of my first year at university were forever life changing. Our roommate committed suicide on a weekend at his parents' home. I experienced health issues with my eyes. I withdrew from my studies multiple times over a relatively short period of time and had several major eye surgeries. I lost vision in one eye and this pushed me deeper into my Red Zone. I was devastated and I really wanted to die. I thought about committing suicide several times. I felt insecure about myself more than ever before. However, I did keep myself alive and eventually returned to university with a heavy heart and even more deflated. I scratched and clawed my way through university and earned two degrees in six years. I graduated with an Honours Bachelor of Mathematics degree and then a Bachelor of Education degree. I was proud of myself for being able to add my designations after my name. I felt more like a somebody that I now have some defined direction in my life. My identity was shaping together. I was a qualified high school teacher who was nervously and anxiously looking forward to starting my teaching career.

I have been a high school Mathematics teacher in Toronto for seventeen years in which I have been Department Head for the last five years. I work in the Green Zone and I deserve it. I bring a Green Zone attitude to work with my colleagues and my students. I am generally well liked and received by both colleagues and students. My experiences as a high school student have shaped me to be a hard working, sensitive, and caring teacher. My wife, Kelly thinks that at times I work too hard especially with all the work that I bring home but I enjoy what I do!

Kelly and I have been married for thirteen years. Our marriage was primarily a Yellow Zone and Red Zone marriage for the first ten years. Kelly and I disagreed, argued, and verbally sparred with each other about a number of issues from my Red Zone family to how to raise our son. We threw accusations back and forth at each other. Our collective behavior was destructive and emotionally bruising to the both of us. Kelly and I sought marriage counseling during the early years of our marriage. I felt inferior around my wife just like I did around my parents. I perceived her as controlling, disrespectful, and angry toward me. We jointly visited Dr. Sohail on a number of occasions over the past number of years. My wife was introduced to the Green Zone, Yellow Zone, and Red Zone concept. She also had individual sessions with Dr. Sohail to discuss how she can help me. Dr. Sohail provided my wife with a lot of insight about my emotional state from childhood to adulthood. He discussed with Kelly ways that she could support me better and where he would like us as a couple and me to be in the future. We knew that we had to work hard together to create a Green Zone marriage and family life. Kelly knew that my frequent visits to Dr. Sohail were helping me be at more peace with myself thus making me a more positive person to be around. Today, our marriage is stable and growing in a lot of ways as our visions for the future are converging. I am very lucky to have a wife like Kelly. She is a caring, passionate, honest, hard working, and very loving woman. She is a very good mother to our son, Nick. Kelly is supportive of my therapy and helps me get out of Red Zone situations. A significant number of these Red Zone situations still relate to my family of origin.

My mother, Sue died over three years ago. Since her death my father and I have developed a superficial Green Zone relationship. I wear my "Emotional Raincoat" when I communicate with my father. We speak on the phone once or twice a month. I usually phone him. He visits my home every few months primarily to visit my son. Our relationship is relatively stable and has peaked like a small mountain. I do not expect any more than that. My father has a Red Zone personality. He likes control. He easily and openly criticizes people if they do something that he does not agree with or they do something without his blessing. He also has a tendency to fabricate stories and ideas. He often deviates from facts in a Red Zone manner. Quite often, his ego dictates his behaviour and thoughts. My father's heavy handed approach has somewhat softened since my mother's death. My father has learned to respect my boundaries. He also has stopped trying to control my marriage and my decision making. Not surprisingly, my wife and my father have had a very rocky and turbulent relationship from the beginning. They have now developed a superficial Green Zone relationship as well.

A few months after my first visit to Dr. Sohail five years ago, my parents were invited by Dr. Sohail to come to his clinic to have a joint session with me. It was a Red Zone session in which I felt that I was having an emotional meltdown. I lost my composure and my anger toward my parents surfaced. I blamed them for creating my Red Zone. On that day I hugged my mother for the last time before her death. Also on that day, I thought that I would never speak to my father again. I was wrong. Living in my Green Zone has allowed me to currently include my father in my life.

Green Zone therapy has taught me that there are two ways to handle a troubled relationship - either to resolve it or to dissolve it. I dissolved my relationship with my brother, Rob and his wife, Carry shortly after our mother's death. Rob has caused me a lot of deep emotional pain since we were young people growing up as brothers in our hometown. He always wants to 'one up' me in almost everything that I do. His competitive and malicious nature has taken me far away from him to the point of dissolution. His Red Zone personality is very similar to my father's. It is interesting that these two Red Zone men share a Green Zone relationship. One notable difference between Rob and myself is that I have chosen to make myself a better person through therapy by creating my Green Zone so that I can become a Green Zone husband, father, teacher, and global citizen. I am honest with myself and acknowledge my shortcomings.

I have a superficially Green Zone relationship with my sister, Ann and her husband, Ray. We communicate with each other by phone or e-mail once to twice a month. We see each other about two to three times per year. My sister has always been very emotionally conservative but also competitive and jealous. Just like my relationship with my father, this relationship has peaked to superficial Green. My sister and I do not have a strong emotional bond but we stay within each other's boundaries. Our relationship is somewhat 'generic' in that we discuss a number of current event topics. On occasion, we talk about family and others that we know. Currently, Ann is not on speaking terms with our father and brother. These relationships seem to be close to being dissolved. My brother-in-law, Ray is a very upfront person who speaks the truth. His truthfulness is the primary reason for these Red Zone relationships existing. My father has asked me to help resolve his relationship with Ann but I refused. I wish to stay in my Green Zone with my family and my "Family of the Heart".

My primary "Family of the Heart" includes Kelly's father Vic, mother Sandy, sister Melanie, her husband Ian, and their son Dave. They have been part of my Green Zone since Kelly and I got married. Kelly's parents live in Alberta. They have always given me more love and respect than a son-in-law could imagine. They treat me like their own son. We see each other in Alberta or in Ontario once or twice per year. They are both very good natured, big hearted, and humble people. They always shower unconditional love on my family especially on Nick. Kelly was raised by her parents generally in a Green Zone environment. Kelly and Melanie are very tightly emotionally bonded with their parents. I envy yet deeply admire their relationship. Melanie and her family live a few minutes from us. Kelly and her sister speak to each other on the phone practically daily. As young sisters growing up in Alberta, Kelly and Melanie were not close. They both coincidentally got married in the same year and both settled in the same Ontario town. They have created a Green Zone environment as sisters, mothers and wives. Melanie is not only a wonderful sister and daughter, she is also a terrific aunt. She loves Nick like her own son. Melanie is also a sister to me. We have had a Green Zone relationship since I have known her. She is a good listener and has always supported my Red Zone struggles with my family of origin and with her sister. Her husband and son are also part of this Green Zone relationship. Melanie and her family are always there for Kelly, Nick, and I in providing all types of support to us.

Kelly's brother Mark lives in Alberta with his daughter, Mia and estranged wife, Jackie. Kelly and I have a Yellow Zone relationship with Mark. He and his family do not have a significant role in our lives.

I feel very fortunate to have Kelly's family in our lives. The love, respect, and emotional support that I receive from them is unparalleled. This support coupled with my therapy has helped me to significantly discover, create, and define my Green Zone. I sincerely thank my Green Zone citizens for helping me live on my Green Zone island in the global Red Sea.

LETTER TO NEIL — CREATING A GREEN ZONE FAMILY

Dear Neil, Thank you for sharing the highlights of your Green Zone Journey. After reading your story I remembered when I first met you, how much your family conflicts were a source of tension and distress for you. It did not take me long to realize that you were brought up in a Red Zone family and community that had undermined your self confidence, self worth and self image. I became aware early in therapy that you were well respected and liked at work and your students and colleagues adored you and made you feel special, but you were not respected and adored in your own family. They did not make you feel special.

Because your parents were in conflict with your wife, you saw them infrequently. I invited your wife and asked her to give you the blessing to see your parents. I mentioned to her that if she did not give her blessing, you might resent her one day, especially when your parents died. I suggested to her that if she did not want to interact with them, you could go and visit them on your own.

After getting your wife's blessing I focused on your relationship with your parents. When I first mentioned that I would like to invite your parents for a family meeting you were shocked. You did not think they would come. After a few months when you felt comfortable with the idea, I called them and invited them for a family meeting. You were surprised that they accepted my invitation. The family meeting was so stressful for you that you walked out in the middle of the session. After a few minutes when you came back, I requested your dad to be respectful to you and connect you with your mom whenever you called. Although you were skeptical, your dad did follow my requests. I shared with you that I treated your dad with due respect so that he could cooperate with me. You did not realize that your parents, as immigrants from Asia, felt comfortable with me as they saw me as an Asian immigrant, too. We spoke the same mother tongue. During that interview I also realized that they loved you but they expressed their love in a traditional Eastern way and you felt controlled by them as you grew up in Canada with Western values. Their mothering was smothering for you. I helped them respect your boundaries. I also realized that you were under a lot of pressure as you were the child of first generation immigrants who had high expectations. Your father, as a teacher and head of a department, wanted the best for you but his dreams had turned into your nightmares. But when I made those boundaries clear he was respectful of my suggestions and that took some pressure off you and you could have a peaceful relationship with them. As your therapist I was amused to see that you chose to be a teacher, like your dad, in the same subject, and now you are the Head of Mathematics Department, like him.

I remember the time when your mom was admitted to the hospital and you had to face your Red Zone brother. You were uncomfortable but you managed. After your mom died you were unsure about your relationship with your dad. Since he treated you with respect, I suggested that you might be able to have a superficial Green Zone relationship with him. When you approached him, he was open for a relationship because he was feeling lonely. I was impressed by your wife as she supported you in your establishing a new relationship with your dad. One of my reasons to encourage your contacts with your dad was because I wanted your son to have a Green Zone loving relationship with your dad, his grandpa. I am a great supporter of a special relationship between grandparents and grandchildren as I had a wonderful loving relationship with my grandparents, sometimes better than my own parents. I am glad that your dad has been a better grandfather than a father.

I am quite impressed that over the years you have resolved some of your family relationships and brought them to your Green Zone and dissolved those relationships that were toxic and in the Red Zone. I think you are fortunate to have wonderful parents-in-law. You have a far better relationship with your wife's parents than your own.

I am so pleased that you have worked hard in your individual, marital and group therapy sessions, creating a Green Zone Family and transforming your stressful Red Zone Lifestyle into a peaceful Green Zone Lifestyle. I am sure many readers will be inspired when they read your struggles and how you over came them. Thanks once again for sharing your Green Zone Story.

Sincerely,

Sohail

Chapter Twelve

An Encounter with Green Zone Living: Witnessing the Unfolding of a Creative Technique in Psychotherapy: From Breakdowns to Breakthroughs
- Mutaal Mooquin

A few decades from now, no book about psychotherapy techniques will be complete without including information about Green Zone Living, a technique conceived and developed by Dr. Khalid Sohail at his clinic in Whitby, Ontario. I knew Dr. Khalid Sohail only as a poet, writer, and humanist activist until I attended a seminar conducted by him and his colleague, Bette Davis about Green Zone Living. To be green these days stamps one as an environmentalist. I am an active environmentalist — in my professional work as well as in my extracurricular activities. So, reading the e-mail about a seminar on

Green Zone Living did not go unnoticed by me. After advocating for so many years green living in our energy use, our waste handling, and our water conservation, an idea about green living in 'mind space' was irresistible.

The information delivered at the seminar and gathered by a brief discussion, a video and a book did not satisfy my curiosity. So, I decided to explore further and asked Dr. Khalid Sohail and Bette Davis for an interview. They gracefully agreed. I wrote this article in order to make the information I gathered easy accessible and to provide an overview of concept and methodology. The idea of Green Zone Living stems from a sincere desire to help people in a dignified way with their emotional and psychological problems and to improve their quality of life. It helps by providing the tools and techniques to apply in day to day life to prevent mental health problems down the road.

Green Zone Living is a creative and unique application of cognitive behavioral therapy (CBT). Though in its entirety it is not limited to cognitive therapy, its emphasis appears to be in that direction. CBT believes that the way we think determines the way we feel. Typically, CBT identifies debilitating or inaccurate emotions and thoughts, in order to influence these behaviors by replacing negative with positive patterns. CBT is widely accepted as an empirical and cost-effective form of psychotherapy. According to *A Guide to Understanding Cognitive and Behavioural Psychotherapies*, "It can be used with groups of people as well as individuals, and the techniques are also commonly adapted for self-help manuals and, increasingly, for self-help software packages."

The point of departure to understanding the uniqueness of Green Zone Living (GZL) is to differentiate it from a typical CBT to which it belongs in a general way. It is the way GZL engages the participant and therapist in a humanistic interaction and the way it focuses on prevention rather than on diagnosis. There are two aspects of this differentiation from CBT: one of technique, the other of underlying principles.

In terms of technique, Dr. Sohail identifies three features. The first one is the way GZL engages the participants in creating self-awareness in their day-to-day life. The technique provides easy tools for that purpose. The basic tool is the concept of being in a Green, Yellow or Red Zone, a symbol taken from our traffic lights. "People are in the Green Zone when they feel relaxed and peaceful and are enjoying their lives. They are in the Yellow Zone when they are a little upset, frustrated or sad, and they are in their Red Zone when they get so angry, distressed and depressed that they start thinking and behaving irrationally." This categorization process helps a person to efficiently recognize his or her state of mind and therefore stop when on a negative course, like one stops for a red signal light.

The second feature is the component of education. In GZL, the therapist does not treat the person as a passive patient but as an active partner in learning more about their unique situation. The participants (please note that I am not using the word 'patient' as the GZL approaches the 'patient' as a participant in self-education) are encouraged to learn and train themselves with or without the help of the therapists to apply the concepts of GZL in their daily lives and to cope with negative situations.

The third distinctive component is the use of writing as a therapeutic tool. With the help of therapists, a structured journal writing technique develops over time in many cases. But typically, the technique is explored to fit individual cases sometimes limited to journal writing. The writing may be shared between participant and therapists or it may remain private. Moreover, writing is not limited to journal writing. It also includes writing letters between therapist and participants or among the participants in case of family or group situation. As writing requires an active approach, practicing it reinforces the concept of cooperative participation by all instead of an approach of passive patient-doctor relationship.

Reflecting on distinct features of this approach, Dr. Sohail expressed the notion that it is a "humanistic" interact between two individuals in the here and now, going to the past only when necessary, and using medication only as a last resort. He says, "My focus is not just on one clinical condition, I want to focus on participant's personality and improve their quality of life. ...Green Zone Philosophy is health and growth oriented rather than illness oriented like traditional medicine and psychiatry."

According to Dr. Sohail, the technique evolved by applying the principles first to himself, then sharing it with friends and family and, finally, bringing it to the clinical practice. This process involved writing four books, making two videos and a website (www.greenzoneliving.ca) and conducting a seminar to introduce it to the public at large.

Before I introduce the distinct features of the underlying principles, I would like to cite an extract from a letter by Dr. Sohail. This will give the reader a glimpse of the man behind this innovative work. "When I was a teenager living in Peshawar, Pakistan, I used to visit all the libraries in town and read books in the literature, religion, philosophy and psychology sections. During those days I used to read Urdu books. One evening I found a 1000-page book on Freud and psychoanalysis. It was so fascinating that I fell in love with the mysteries of the human mind and decided that I will pursue my future unraveling those mysteries and serving people who suffer from emotional problems and mental illness. It is my professional attempt to transform breakdowns into breakthroughs. I believe in life long learning. I am far more transparent with my patients than most therapists I know. I tell my patients that I learn as much from them as they learn from me. I thank them for trusting me and sharing their life stories."

Let us now explore the underlying principles. Unique in psychotherapy practice, GZL incorporates the principles of diverse schools of thought in a flexible manner. The most prevalent schools are: Intra-psychic principles of Psychoanalysis, principles of Interpersonal school of Harry Stack Sullivan, Humanistic principles of Third Force or Humanistic psychology; principles of Murray Bowen's Family System Theory, Sartreian existential approach and Victor Frankl's Logo-therapy. However, clearly, work on the 'floor' and its application in the clinic and in self-help superseded the conceptual or research work in a laboratory.

Any account of threads woven into the organic whole of GZL must start with Psychoanalysis founded by Sigmund Freud. Dr. Sohail becomes very animated when talking about Freud and his ideas. One can spend hours listening him talk about it. His passion stems from the fact that Freud so ably used scientific approach in unraveling the mysteries of mind — discovering and formulating the workings of the 'subconscious' — the great iceberg whose tiny tip is the 'conscious'. "I was most intrigued by the defense mechanism of Rationalization stating that many human behaviors are inspired by unconscious motives but later on, our mind creates a rational explanation for irrational acts."

But since Psychoanalysis can be a lengthy process, according to Dr. Sohail, he studied and incorporated techniques of Peter Sifneos and Habib Davanloo who developed Short Term Dynamic Psychotherapy. This treatment approach accomplishes in a few months what takes classical psychoanalysis years. In addition, psychoanalysis has its limitation and can be helpful only in certain situations. That is where the interpersonal approach of Harry Stack Sullivan opens up the other vistas. Sullivan considered anxiety a result of conflicted interpersonal relationships and low self esteem. His ideas of "Good me, Bad Me and Not Me" are at the core of the Sullivanian approach. "Receiving positive feedback fosters positive attitudes and so is the reverse. Bad becomes so big that it breaks down the self generating disintegration of personality."

The next expansion to the GZL approach was the adaptation of Murray Bowen Systems Theory to Family Therapy. According to this approach the "basic unit of human relationship is a triangle." Dr. Sohail says, "After discovering the concept of triangulation I realized why in some situations of marital therapy I was not successful because one spouse perceived me as siding with the other spouse and both of us ganging up on her/him. When I feel that one spouse is having difficulties trusting me, I invite my co-therapist, Bette Davis to balance the triangulation."

Through this evolution of a "wholistic" approach, the incorporation of Victor Frank's Logotherapy, Abraham Maslow's humanism and Eric Fomm's integration of a cultural approach were a natural progression. Frankl's logo-therapy is based on the idea that human sufferings become more bearable if they find a meaning in a person's life, while Maslow focused more on "healthy people especially those who had reached the heights of their personal, professional and creative growth … the self-actualized people." Eric Fromm's approach incorporates the effects of cultures on human development. His ideas were of great significance for Dr. Sohail to understand trans-cultural conflicts to which immigrants are subjected.

The account of GZL cannot be complete without describing the influence of Albert Ellis who "is generally considered to be one of the originators of the cognitive revolutionary paradigm shift in psychotherapy and the founder of cognitive behavioral therapies" According to Dr. Sohail, "Bette Davis has a keen interest in that philosophy and I have learnt a lot about Rational Emotive Therapy from her. Being a co-therapist she has been a great asset to our clinic. She has also helped me in creating books and producing videos on Green Zone."

This brought our conversation towards the working of the clinic itself. "After working in psychiatric hospitals for two decades I decided to start my Creative Psychotherapy Clinic in 1995 with the help of Anne Henderson to develop my own model. Green Zone Therapy has been a gradual evolution of my philosophy and practice. Alongside learning from all these philosophers I have added my own flavor to the practice."

Here is a brief summary of the seven steps that according to GZL can lead to a healthy, happy and peaceful lifestyle.

Step 1: Become aware of your Three Zones of living: Green, Yellow and Red. The visual metaphor of traffic lights provides an easy anchor point to categorize and work upon your emotional states. These are tools to facilitate awareness of self communication with others.

Steps 2 - 4: The Three Rs: Recognize the changes in Emotional Zones; Recover from Yellow and Red Zones; and Restrain from going back to Yellow and Red Zones. These steps "help people learn not to react to other people's Yellow and Red Zones. In this way people identify their triggers and then they find healthy ways to deal with them."

Step 5: Create Green Zone Relationships. In some cases you may need to find "a mediator that can be a friend, relative, minister or a therapist to bring back your relationship into your Green Zone ".

Step 6: Create a Green Zone Social Environment. This includes creating a healthy environment in your family, schools, job, business or social organizations. This may involve developing an Emotional Raincoat (for example, finding support with a group of like-minded people) to cope with Red Zone toxicity until you find healthier alternatives.

Step 7: Create a Green Zone Lifestyle. Discover your special gift by starting with a daily Green Zone Hour. Get in touch with your Natural Self and do things you like to, want to and love to do. Examples are hobbies for which you feel passionate; volunteer work to contribute to the community.

These steps may appear plain and straightforward. In application, they grow rich in content and sophisticated in form. They are no less than guide posts on the long trail of self-discovery. The hallmark of this approach is the attitude displayed towards the people with emotional problems. This approach is reflected in Dr. Sohail's positive words showing respect towards others and a conviction in the power of self healing, "What is important is to see the human being behind the suffering. It is important to shift the focus from "what is wrong with you" to "how great the potential you have". Quoting once again Dr. Sohail, the founder of GZL, "… In every person there is a centre and at the core of this centre is the Green Zone. There is this healthy part within every self - the Green Zone of a person. [Unfortunately] that Green Zone is often pushed away by the Yellow and Red of the social environment. … Often it can be recovered and reclaimed by a person's own activism using the principles of Green Zone Living, sometime with and sometime without outside help."

Part Three

A Fictional Green Zone Story

Chapter Thirteen

River

Darvesh has gone in search of himself.
Sohail

....
(1)
....

One morning I woke up
And looked in the mirror
I did not like what I saw
Not only did I not like,
Rather I hated what I saw
There were subtle changes
So subtle others could not see
But not subtle enough that I could ignore
I was losing my valor
I was losing my vigor
I was losing my figure
The shine in my eyes was decreasing
The doubt in my heart was increasing
I knew it was the beginning of a breakdown
And I knew it well
I was aware
How I would slide down a slippery slope
And would not be able to stop

I knew
How I would hit rock bottom
It was all very familiar
Because I had experienced it before

………………………………..………………...
(2)
………………………………………………..

With the passage of time
I started losing
My confidence
My faith
My optimism
The sun in my heart
Hid behind the clouds
And it became dark, very dark
I became emotionally paralyzed
        Intellectually anaesthetized
I could not focus on my dialogues
I could not concentrate on my discussions
I started forgetting my appointments
My appointments became my disappointments
My staff were shocked
The day I cried like a baby
The more I tried, the worse it got
Finally I had to accept
I could not work anymore
I was sad
I was melancholic
I felt ashamed
I felt embarrassed
I felt guilty

Dr. K. Sohail/Bette Davis

I had to say goodbye to my clients and colleagues
While I was trying to cope with my failing business
My sweetheart told me
She did not love me anymore
I was heartbroken
The more I tried to bring her closer
The more I pushed her away
Within a few months
I lost my house
I lost my spouse
I lost my clients
I lost my colleagues
From a big half million dollar house
I moved to a small basement apartment
Feeling like an utter failure
The worst I ever felt in my life
I was lost
I was confused
I was a traveler
With no dream, no destination
I was a sheep
Who had lost his herd
I was a bird
Who had lost her flock
I felt helpless and hopeless
My life became purposeless and meaningless
I had no reason to live
I had every reason to die
I became suicidal
I asked myself
How would I die?
Take an overdose
Jump off a bridge
Use a shot-gun

I thought and thought
But did not do anything
My worst fear was
I would end up brain damaged
In a wheelchair
In an institution
For the rest of my life
I would become a vegetable
When I lost faith in myself
I also lost faith
 In my friends
          In my family
          In my church
          In my God
I became an agnostic, a skeptic, a doubter
I started doubting everything
          My ideas
          My ideals
          My dreams
          My very existence
          My creativity
          My integrity
          My sanity
          My humanity
I once was solid like a rock
Within a few months
I transformed into sand

....
(3)
...............................…...........................

One evening
When I was getting drunk
In a local pub
A stranger
Sitting on the next stool
Said to me
"You are drowning your sorrows in alcohol
Come with me tomorrow
I will take you
To Wisdom Island
To the Darvesh's Hut"
"Who lives there?"
 I was curious
"A wise couple
Khizr, the wise man
Sophia, the wise woman"
"What is so special there?"
I was intrigued
"They have a healing circle, a Green Zone Circle.
You need healing
You need to be part of that circle"
So the next day
I joined the stranger
Who was more than a friend
In a boat
To Wisdom Island
To the Darvesh's Hut
Next to a lighthouse
Where
Khizr, the wise man from the East
And

Sophia, the wise woman from the West
Led a healing circle
They complemented each other
Like Yin Yang
I joined the Green Zone Circle
The healing circle
And before the meeting ended
A wave of peace embraced me.
In that circle
There was a candle
And only one person spoke at a time
The person holding the candle
Everybody else listened wholeheartedly
And responded compassionately
In the Green Zone Circle
When I heard about
Green, Yellow and Red Zones
I asked Khizr, the wise man
"What is the Green Zone?"
He smiled gracefully and said
"We all have a centre inside us
That centre is the Green Zone
When we are in touch with our center
We get in touch
With our love
With our compassion
With our peace
With our inner wisdom
When we start moving away from the center
We become
Anxious and angry
Nervous and scared
Because we enter our Yellow Zone
And when we completely lose touch with the center

Dr. K. Sohail/Bette Davis

We become agitated and restless
Irritable and irrational
Violent and self destructive
That is when we are in our Red Zone.
In the Green Zone Circle
People help each other
To get in touch with their center
With their peaceful Green Zone
You are more than welcome to join the healing circle.
That day
When I spoke
Sophia, the wise woman
Listened to my story
Smiled gracefully
And said
"All your life you have been climbing the middle class ladder,
A nice profession
A nice house
A loving spouse
A beautiful car
An expensive cottage
A fine boat
And when you reached the top of the ladder
You realized you had been climbing the wrong ladder"
"What is your advice?"
I inquired
"I do not give any advice
I help people realize
It is less important what they *have*
It is more important who they *are*
It is our creativity and integrity that matters
We are all born with special gifts

We need to discover them
Share them with others
Serve humanity
And feel proud of who we are
When people do not like who they *are*
They try to compensate with what they *have*
Their worldly possessions
Unfortunately it does not work
A hole inside the heart
Cannot be filled with outside things
It is like putting water in a sieve
No matter how much water you put in
The sieve always remains thirsty
A heart can be filled only with inner peace
Not with outer worldly possessions"
After that day
I went to Wisdom Island
Every week
Sat in the Green Zone Circle
Listened to the struggles of people
And the sage advice
Of Khizr, the wise man of the East
And Sophia, the wise woman of the West
It helped me heal
It helped me recover
It filled my heart
It filled my mind
With love and compassion
With wisdom and peace
The more I attended the Green Zone Circle
And listened to people's dilemmas and dreams
The more I realized
We are all
Our own worst enemies

Dr. K. Sohail/Bette Davis

But with some
Introspection and reflection
Counsel and compassion
We can become our own best friends
Those who get disillusioned
With the highways of tradition
Must discover
The trails of their hearts
To lead a peaceful life.

....
(4)
....
One day I asked Khizr,
"When does peaceful Green Zone communication
take place?"
The wise man
Was silent for the longest time
And then said
"Mostly in silence
When two people love each other
Sometimes in conversation
When two people respect each other
And when both parties are in the Green Zone
Communication is far more than conversation"
And then he said,
"There are as many truths as human beings
And as many realities as pairs of eyes
In this world
We need to respect each other's truth
Even when we disagree"
Gradually I realized

Each time I met
Khizr, the wise man
Sophia, the wise woman
I learnt something
I felt relaxed
I felt healed
I felt peaceful
I felt wiser
It was a miracle
A healing miracle
A human miracle

....
(5)
....

One day
I shared
With Sophia, the wise woman
I was struggling too much
I was hurting too much
I was too much in pain
She touched me gently and said,
"You are having labor pains
You are giving birth
To your new self
You are breaking down invisible chains"
"What chains?" I asked
"Invisible chains of your childhood conditioning
Your self-judgments
Once you break those chains
You will be free
Like a bird
Like a fish

Dr. K. Sohail/Bette Davis

Like a cool breeze"
She shared the story
Of a big elephant in the zoo
Who could not play
With other elephants
As he was tied
To a tree
With a small chain
A small chain
Put around his leg
When he was very small
Since he could not break the chain
As a child
He believed
He could not break it
As an adult
He was tied
To his past
By his childhood conditioning
And then
One day
There was a fire in the zoo
When all the animals ran
He ran too
And broke the chain
The crisis liberated him
Sophia, the wise woman said,
"You are breaking the chain
To set yourself free
From your traditional middle class values"
As I heard her thoughts
I felt calm and peaceful

....
(6)
....

One morning
Khizr, the wise man said
"After you experience a breakthrough
You will be able
To experience deep love"
"What is deep love?" I asked
He said,
"Let me explain with an example.
In villages
People dig wells
To have water
Some wells are superficial
Water appears at a few feet
Such water
Is good to wash clothes
But not good enough to drink
As it is full of impurities
Sometimes villagers dig twenty to thirty feet deep
To get to deeper water
That water
Is pure
And good enough to drink"
Khizr, the wise man said,
"The human heart
Has two kinds of love
Superficial love
That is emotional and romantic
Full of ego and pride
Full of anxieties and insecurities and jealousies
And deep love
That is magical and mystical and peaceful

Superficial love
Is like a candle in the house
Serving only the dear ones
Deep love
Is like the moon
Serving all of humanity
Many people go through
A crisis
A breakdown
A breakthrough
To get in touch with deep love"
Khizr, the wise man
Consoled me
Comforted me
Reassured me
He said,
" It is a painful process
But in the end
It is all worth it"
His wise words
Were calming and reassuring
It was as if
He was holding my hand
As I was descending
Into the dark recesses of my heart and mind
To find inner light,
The light
That was part of enlightenment.

....
(7)
....

One evening I asked Khizr, the wise man
What is the secret of human growth?
He stared into space for a while and then said,
"Humanity is evolving
From the religious to the spiritual
From the spiritual to the scientific"
"How is a mystic different than a scientist?"
My curiosity asked
"A mystic sees with the inner eye
A scientist proves to the outer eye
A mystic uses intuition
A scientist uses intelligence
A mystic has a compassionate heart
A scientist has a critical mind.
Every mystic is not a scientist
But every scientist is a mystic
He has to imagine with the inner eye
Before he can prove with the naked eye
She has to see it intuitively
Before she can prove it logically"
"Do they complement or contradict?"
I wanted to know
"Only a mystic and a scientist
With bad conscience
Contradict each other
Their egos are more important than truth.
On the other hand
A mystic and a scientist
With good conscience
Complement each other
For them

Dr. K. Sohail/Bette Davis

Truth is more important than their egos
Their truth makes them humble not arrogant
They help people discover
The mysteries of life

....

(8)

....

As weeks and months passed
My savings ran out
As my pocket became empty
My heart became full
One day I realized
I had no money
For food
For rent
For clothes
For travel
One evening I realized
I was the poorest
But the most peaceful
I had ever been
I had nothing to lose
But everything to gain
That night
I slept like a baby
And I had a dream
In that dream
I was sitting next to the lake
The lake was so calm
I could see the reflection of the full moon
It was a wonderful dream
It was a peaceful dream

The next day I shared the dream with the wise ones
They both smiled and said
"Now you are ready
Ready to become a darvesh, a mystic traveler
If you wish you can work for us
We will pay you for your services"
I realized
When one door closes
The other door opens
Unexpectedly
Mysteriously
Magically
That day I found out
Khizr and Sophia
Had a circle of darveshes
Mystic travelers all over the world
Following a special mission
To serve humanity
And help it grow
To the next stage of evolution
I accepted the responsibility
And started traveling around the world
From the West to the East
From the North to the South
In the next few years
I collected wisdom literature
Of the mystics and artists and scientists
I collected the writings of
Bulley Shah and Kabir Das from Asia
Charles Darwin and Albert Einstein from Europe
Chief Seattle and Walt Whitman from America
And many more
Poets and philosophers and scholars
From all over the world

And got their writings translated
Into different languages
And distributed
To the four corners of the world
For the next few years
I traveled a lot
And met men and women
From different communities and cultures
It made me happy
To see them happy
Living with love and peace and harmony
It made me sad
To see them sad
Living with prejudice and violence and war
The more I traveled
The more I realized
That even
After thousands of years of evolution
We, as human beings
Have not learnt
To live peacefully with each other
We still have a tribal mentality
We have not realized
We are all Children of Mother Earth
She brings us into this world
From her womb when we are born
And takes us back into her womb when we die
It was inspiring to see
The more people read wisdom literature
The wiser they became
And became peaceful Green Zone Islands
In violent Red Zone Seas
After I gained inner peace and wisdom
I was surprised to see

Fame and fortune kissed my feet too
I realized
Wealth was like a shadow
When I was pursuing it
It was moving away from me
And when I started moving away from it
It started following me
I was reluctant in the beginning
But after a while
I started accepting and embracing it

....

(9)

....

Once I came back from a long trip
And shared my adventures with Khizr and Sophia
They gave me honest feedback and said
"When you first arrived here
You were a restless materialist
Now you have become a peaceful mystic"
I smiled and said,
"In the last few years
I have found all the things I had lost
A beautiful house
A loving spouse
A sports car
An expensive cottage
A speedy boat
On the surface it all looks the same
What do you think is the difference?"
They both smiled and said,
"The difference is in the type of attachment.
It is like a boat's relationship with the sea

When the water is outside,
The boat is safe
When the water is inside,
The boat is unsafe,
It can be even dangerous
When you first came here
You were a materialist
Your possessions were inside your heart
Now your possessions are outside your heart
Now you enjoy them
But you are not attached to them
If you lose them
You will not have a breakdown
Your inside is no longer controlled by your outside"
When they said those wise words
 I realized
My breakdown had transformed into a breakthrough.

…………………………….………………..
(10)
……………………………….…………..
I finally became aware
Everything is temporary
Everything is transitory
Things come and things go
Life is like a river, let it flow.

Publications from the Green Zone library

<u>Books</u>

Love, Sex, and Marriage

      - Dr. K. Sohail and Bette Davis RN BN MN

The Art of Living in Your Green Zone

The Art of Loving in Your Green Zone

The Art of Working in Your Green Zone

      - Dr. K. Sohail and Bette Davis RN BN MN

Creating Green Zone Schools – The Art of

      Learning in Your Green Zone

      - Dr. K. Sohail and Bette Davis RN BN MN

Green Zone Living - 7 Steps to a Happy, Healthy

      & Peaceful Lifestyle

      - Dr. K. Sohail and Bette Davis RN BN MN

From Islam to Secular Humanism

The Myth of the Chosen One

Prophets of Violence, Prophets of Peace

The Next Stage of Human Evolution

Love Letters to Humanity

Dr. K. Sohail/Bette Davis

Green Zone Publishing

213 Byron Street South

Whitby Ontario Canada L1N4P7

Please contact us through our website at

www.greenzoneliving.ca

www.ingramcontent.com/pod-product-compliance
Lightning Source LLC
Chambersburg PA
CBHW031139270326
41931CB00028B/786